DISCOVER YOUR GREATNESS

An Innovative 8-Step Power Planning Process that Unlocks the Power of Your Heart and Unleashes Your Unique Greatness

TIM REDMOND

insight
PUBLISHING GROUP

Tulsa, Oklahoma

DISCOVER YOUR GREATNESS
© 2009 by Tim Redmond

Published by Insight Publishing Group
8801 S. Yale, Suite 410
Tulsa, OK 74137
918-493-1718

Unless otherwise indicated, all Scripture quotations are taken from the Holy Bible, New Living Translation, copyright © 1996, 2004. Used by permission of Tyndale House Publishers, Inc., Wheaton, IL 60189. All rights reserved.

ISBN 978-1932503-84-5
Library of Congress catalog card number: 2009928296

Printed in the United States of America

Contents

A Personal Word from Tim Redmond

This is a great day for you! Thank you for investing in this book. I am confident it will prove to be a rewarding use of your time and focus.

You are a leader filled with unique God-given abilities that will create lasting impact in the lives of countless people. This book is designed to wake up and employ the creative power within you using a unique process that will prove to significantly increase the results you are after.

Your assignment and especially the people attached to that assignment are too wonderful and fulfilling to be ignored.

Because of that, I wrote this book.

It is designed to be a training manual. You will reap far greater rewards when you involve yourself with the stories and principles and respond to the carefully selected questions.

One of the most unselfish things leaders do is invest in themselves. That's exactly the attitude to have when reading through this book. Invest in yourself by taking time to answer the questions honestly with all of your heart present. Set a date with your destiny by investing time to fill out the downloadable power planning tools available with the purchase of this book.

Doing so will expand your future and enable you to better enjoy the journey along the way!

We'll start our journey with a personal experience that clarified and activated these powerful planning principles in my life. . .

From Zero to Over $100 Million...

What was I doing moving from a secure, prestigious job at Coopers & Lybrand (now PriceWaterhouseCoopers) to a fledgling high tech start-up company?

There were just two of us and our assistant. Typical start up – all of us did everything. No guarantees of success – only the challenge of maneuvering in uncharted waters.

Yet my heart pulsated with expectation. I had just celebrated my 26th birthday and I had my whole life ahead of me. In college, I always told myself that I didn't want to climb the corporate latter; I wanted to build one.

With as much focus as a 20-something could muster, I wrote a vision full of outrageous goals and milestones to reach. Amazingly, nearly every one of those seemingly impossible goals were reached! When we eventually sold the business to a Fortune 500 company, we had over 400 employees working at the company producing almost $40 million in annual sales. Including the selling of the company, we generated over $100 million in pre-tax profits!

How did we enjoy so much success? By mastering and implementing the powerful principles contained in this book. You hold in your hand the key to propel your future forward in ways you may have never imagined.

If you have had challenges in creating compelling, heart-felt plans that generates amazing energy from within, this book is going to give you the confidence to pursue the planning process – for your personal life and for your business or organization.

The key to building unshakeable confidence begins with examining and deliberating the foundation principle that determines the fate of any plan or goal. It is the lever that moves the world . . .

What Do You Believe?
5 Essential Realities

All effective plans and goals begin with faith. Achieving significant results through this unique planning process requires believing these five essential realities about who you really are (written in the first person so you can say them aloud to yourself):

1. I am designed and filled with the ability to dream and create. I am made in the image of God the Creator – He wired me to operate and create as He does. What I have on the inside of me right now is enough to change, improve and create what I desire on the outside.

2. ALL things are possible to me and I am a powerful person. The dream and plan I have on the inside of me is possible and will happen!

3. Regardless of what has happened in my past and what is going on in my present situation, my future is bigger and better. My future IS bigger than my past!

4. Effective planning begins with the mindset of abundance. Wealth and abundance are everywhere and can be created in any circumstance I face. My mindset of abundance opens my eyes to see opportunities, key relationships and processes that I would be blind to otherwise.

5. The planning process is a positively powerful process and is the point where I begin to create.

STOP! Think about what you just read!

Do you really believe each of these five realities? Did you just glance over them and are ready to get to the "more important" steps in this planning process? Or did your heart resonate and get energized with these truths?

What you believe – especially about yourself – creates your future.

Whatever you most deeply believe begins to show up in your life in some way. Your beliefs are the lever that multiplies the strength to launch your plans into reality. The closer your beliefs are to your plan, the more power you'll have to execute the plan and reach your goal.

Jesus said, "ALL things are possible to him who believes." This is one of the most powerful statements I've ever read. As C.S. Lewis said, "Jesus is either a lying lunatic or he is telling the truth."

"All things" . . . except for your situation, correct? Absolutely not! When He said all things, He was also referring to YOUR plans, dreams and goals.

". . . are possible to him that believes." That's the power of your beliefs!

That's why I am emphasizing the important role your beliefs play at the beginning of this powerful planning process.

If all things are possible when I believe, what does it mean to believe?

In short, believing consists of 3 parts. It is what you . . .

1. SEE. It is something you see (on the inside of you).

2. ARE CERTAIN OF. It is something you are totally convinced or certain of is true.

3. TAKE ACTIONS TOWARDS. Because you are so convinced of what you see on the inside, you think, feel, decide and act in line with that belief.

This is the way you are wired. That's why Jesus focused on what a person believed (or had faith for – it's the same thing) BEFORE He helped them. Your results on the outside are created by what you believe on the inside.

The first part of planning is making sure your beliefs are in line with the plan; otherwise you will give up or sabotage the plan. You will never go higher than you think or believe.

What if you dreamed of running a highly successful business but you have a belief that is contrary to it? Let's say you are currently working in a lower level job and really believe you don't have what it takes to get promoted to the highest ranks in the company.

Even if you have the best plan in the world, how are you going to respond when faced with tough decisions and challenging situations?

What if you believed you had what it took and were worthy of long term success? Even if it didn't appear promising, each obstacle would be an encouragement for you to learn and improve, study, and build relationships with mentors. With these beliefs, instead of avoiding difficult assignments, you will be more likely to dive into them, knowing they are equipping you to fulfill your dream.

Jesus made another profound statement, "these signs will follow them that believe." He then listed a number of signs that their beliefs would produce.

What do signs follow? This is a profound concept about the power of your beliefs!

Signs follow beliefs. Beliefs produce signs. The inside determines the outside.

The outside follows what is on the inside of you.

To put it another way, the ongoing or reoccurring signs in your life are indicative of what you most deeply believe.

What are signs?

Another word for signs is results.

The results that follow your beliefs can be those that Jesus mentioned in Mark 16. They can also be the way you respond and react to others. Signs can be the decisions you make, thought patterns you think and even the emotions you feel. Your most deeply held beliefs dictate your behavior and create the results in your life.

Your most deeply held beliefs dictate your behavior and create the results in your life.

Let's say you lost your wallet and didn't know it until the end of the day. In the middle of the day, you don't believe (see, are certain of and take action towards) you lost it – you don't even know you don't have it! You are having a great day – thinking positively, feeling great and whistling while you work.

What happens when you become aware of your missing wallet? Immediately your thoughts, feelings and actions follow that belief. You think of all the money you lost and the hassle of replacing all of your valuables in the wallet. You feel dreadful and are suffering from a panic attack. You immediately begin retracing your steps, looking feverishly for your lost wallet. You believe you lost your wallet.

Then the reality hits you. You didn't lose your wallet; you simply left it on the dresser on your way out the door that morning. What then happens to your thoughts, feelings and actions? They change again – this time in line with your new reality or belief.

Here is another way of seeing it. Beliefs are your leaders. So what follows your beliefs? Feelings follow. Thoughts follow. Decisions follow. Behaviors follow (your responses and reactions).

Signs indicate what you really believe; not what you WANT to believe. That's why I am urging you to stop and consider what you really believe. Does it line up with the 5 realities listed earlier?

What "signs" follow your life? Do you like them? The signs in your life change when your beliefs do.

How do you change your beliefs?

This is a BIG topic and one that is outside the scope of this book (it is covered in detail in the *Emotions of Money* CD Seminar. However, here are a few thoughts that will help.

Changing a belief is really changing what and how you see on the inside of you. Beliefs are really the controlling or dominant images in your heart that you are convinced are true. They are the movies or pictures you play over and over on the inside of you. In them, you see yourself succeeding or failing, winning or losing, overcoming or being a victim. As it says in Proverbs, "as a man thinks in his heart, so is he."

Change your images by changing what and how you see. By REPEATEDLY filling your thoughts, eyes and ears with the right images, you'll begin to replace your driving, dominant images (those that control you and create your results). How you see yourself is also influenced by the words you speak (especially words you say to yourself about yourself) and behaviors you take.

I recommend declaring these 5 realities aloud (with passion!) at the start, middle and end of your day for the next several days.

If your current beliefs are different from these, get ready for a battle! Your old, defeating beliefs will fight to survive. They'll use logic, past experiences, and uncomfortable feelings to get you to relieve the pressure to destroy and replace them.

Don't give up or give in to the paralyzing beliefs that distort the creative power already resident in you.

Remember, most things change in a state of discomfort. Be aware of the deceptive addiction of comfort and status quo and press through the initial discomfort of changing your beliefs.

Stay committed to deliberately filling your mind and mouth with the affirming truths about who you are and watch your dreaming and planning capacities expand!

It is crucial to begin this planning process being fully convinced of these 5 realities. I suggest you take a moment right now and say them again – this time with even MORE passion and focus!

The intensity of emotion you use when declaring these truths will act as a tattoo to the deepest part of your being. The greater the intensity, the deeper and more permanent the tattoo.

Dr. Albert Mehrabian, Professor Emeritus of Psychology at UCLA studied communication and found that when communicating about emotional issues (your plans and goals are emotional!), only 7% of the actual message communicated was verbal. He found that 38 percent of the credibility of the message was vocal (volume, pitch, rhythm, etc) and 55 percent was posture and facial expressions.

The intensity of emotion you use when declaring these truths will act as a tattoo to the deepest part of your being.

What does this mean to you? When you declare these truths, don't just say words. Declare them with strength, volume and intense positive emotion. Stand tall with your shoulders straight and your face full of confidence and certainty.

Feelings are followers. Regardless of how you feel when you begin declaring them, your feelings will follow the confidence and authority of your tone and posture. When you speak from a strong emotional state, your ability to create increases.

With your key beliefs in place, it is time to remove the apprehension frequently attached to the planning process. By clearly seeing the spiritual side of planning and embracing the benefits from this powerful process, you are well on your way to creating massive results . . .

Why Take Time to Plan?

It's an easy thing to convince yourself to avoid planning UNLESS you are more convinced of the benefits. Here are just some of the amazing outcomes you can expect:

1. Planning releases you to live your life without regrets!

Towards the end of their life, many people are pained with regrets. What regrets have you heard people say? What regrets do you want to avoid having towards the end of YOUR life?

Planning in the way that I teach it will set you up so that you can live your life without regrets.

Daniel Burnham built America's first skyscraper. He said, "Make no little plans. There's nothing in little plans to stir men's blood. Make big plans. Once a big idea is recorded, it can never die."

2. Planning increases your wealth creation capacities.

God has given you a *Unique Power to Create Wealth*. Effective plans release the energy and greatness of that power to impart value into the lives of others. Wealth is created and the outside world begins to conform to the heart-birthed plan on the inside of you. This is "living by faith" and becomes the vehicle with which to release your faith to create an ever-expanding future.

Heart-birthed plans attract what is needed to achieve the plan. Needs, by themselves (without being attached to an effective plan), do NOT attract resources.

3. Planning helps you stay focused and highly motivated.

Consider the power of focus: What you focus on, you move towards (and it moves towards you), especially your plan!

Life offers so many distractions, many of which appeal to our egos and talents. Planning and goal achieving gives you the power to say, "NO!" to these "greatness" blockers. A heart-birthed plan steadies the path of your purpose, right relationships, priorities and activities.

The focus that a plan brings guides you in the best use of your time. The secret of the super successful is how they use their time – especially what they do with their spare time. Focus brings balance.

4.   Planning leads to better decision-making.

Your decisions determine your destiny – your success and failure comes as a result of the decisions you make. Your life – and the results you see in your life are a result of ALL the decisions you've made in life so far.

Planning is a process of identifying and pursuing your personal and organizational purpose, key goals, and values. It is committing to a number of decisions in advance. This is especially helpful when you are confused and not sure what direction to take.

The benefits of planning far outweigh any pain or fear that have stopped you in the past. Let's understand why so many have shied away from the planning process before we delve into the 8 Power Planning Principles. . .

Why So Many Shy Away from Planning

Planning is an area in which so many powerful people with huge destinies fall short. It doesn't have to be that way!

Planning is really about making clear the target you are aiming at and moving and adjusting towards it until you reach it.

Have you made any goals or plans for this year? Do you actively do this each year and throughout the year?

If so, I congratulate you! You are tapping into your God-given power to create huge results. . .

Have you had a negative experience when setting goals and making plans?

People get disillusioned and discouraged when thinking about planning and goal setting for a number of reasons, some of which include –

1. **Busyness.** Being so busy with life, they don't take time to focus on what they really want or if they do, they forget about goals they set.

2. **Fear of Failure**. Why try when they are convinced they're going to fail? (Sounds like a belief that needs to be rooted out and replaced.)

3. **Lack of Confidence**. They are convinced they don't have what it takes and are uncomfortable with being held accountable to pre-determined results and actions.

4. **Overwhelmed**. They try to set too many goals at one time and get overloaded with them – there are too many objectives to focus upon. The narrower your focus, the greater your passion.

5. **Ignorance**. They simply don't know how to plan and achieve goals effectively.

If you have struggled with any of these, today is a great day for you. I'm going to show you a powerful, fun, and easy way to get into the Power Planning process in a massively effective way. Through the principles and examples that I will share, you will overcome each of these five roadblocks in the planning process.

This approach will also help you discover the greatness within you and release it in a powerful, creative way that produces huge results!

If you are comfortable with the planning and goal setting process, I'm going to give you a new and very possibly, more effective way to begin this process.

Planning Principle 1 that is covered in the next chapter provides one of the most significant benefits of my unique planning system...

Power Planning Principle 1:
The Power is in the Pursuit

Planning with its related action items gives you a target to shoot for. Your faith and the unique greatness inside of you require a target, a goal, a plan to aim at to be fully utilized.

God created and wired you to be successful. I call that internal wiring your Internal Success System. If we don't give our Internal Success System something to aim towards, it becomes weak and ineffective.

John Goddard at 15 wrote down 127 goals he wanted to reach during his lifetime.[1] At the time I read his story, he had already reached 108 of those goals – some of them included climbing the highest mountains, visiting the most primitive cultures, and reading the world's best books.

John's "Goal List" expands the hearts of those who read it. What is important to note is that he gave his Internal Success System a target to shoot for. He gave himself a goal to reach and a destination to pursue. This is crucial in the planning and goal-achieving process.

It is fulfilling to achieve your goals and reach your desired destination.

Yet in the Kingdom of God, the planning process provides something even more important than achieving the target.

Although this may seem strange to you, reaching the destination is NOT the most important thing. What is the most important aspect of this process?

It is the development of your heart.

Your heart is the focal point of the whole kingdom of God. In the Parable of the Sower, Jesus said that this parable is the key to understanding all of the other parables relating to the Kingdom of God. The lesson of this cornerstone story is effectiveness of the seed or the Word is dependent upon the quality of the soil.

What is the "soil" being referred to here? The soil is our hearts. If the heart is the focal point of the whole Kingdom, it should be the focal point of your planning process. It is the development of our heart that we are focused on with all of our planning and goal setting.

It is in the pursuit of your goals that your heart wakes up and releases its greatness.

It is in the pursuit of your goals and plans that your heart is developed. As Zig Zigler said, "Remember, what you get by reaching your destination isn't nearly as important as what you become by reaching your goals – what you will become is the winner you were born to be!" This was Albert Hubbard's focus when he said, "we work to become, not to acquire."

As you pursue your goals, opportunities are created to develop and strengthen relationships, overcome obstacles, and improve your skills.

It is in the pursuit of your goals that your heart wakes up and releases its greatness. In the active pursuit of your plans and goals, you become all you can be.

Committing to and implementing your plans and your goals sets in motion the Law of Attraction.

What is the Law of Attraction?

Whatever you are focused on, deeply committed to and begin to pursue, a magnetic force field is created around your life to attract all that is necessary to accomplish that goal. It attracts resources, ideas, strategies, skills and the right people into your life to help you achieve what you set out to do. That is part of the power of your Internal Success System.

Here is another thought related to this that most do NOT consider. Your plans and goals may ALSO attract obstacles, challenges and resistance into your life.

You will have certain challenges come into your life when you begin to implement your plans and goals that you would NOT have if you didn't begin to pursue your plans.

This is why people get scared away from this powerful process. The internal changes that are required to adapt and overcome come at a price tag greater than they want to pay. (The addiction to comfort devours your personal development like a cancer. God gave us a Comforter because He knew we would need comfort in the pursuit of our assignment!)

Have you ever responded this way to challenges?

What is your response when you have challenges and obstacles? Do you run away? Do you say that your plans will never come to pass? Do you get depressed and disappointed? Do you start blaming and accusing everyone and everything around you?

Your response to all of these questions is "NO!" Consider what James is saying in the first chapter of his life-changing book.

You count it ALL joy because you have a completely different way of looking at obstacles. First of all, you're not surprised when they come. You know that your plan is so full of God's will that it will get resist-ance.

But that resistance is a necessary part of the pursuit of your goal – it helps you become bigger, better, more compassionate, more skillful, and wiser in the process. The challenges that your plan attracts develop your heart so that you become strong enough to keep moving forward when you are tempted to give up!

This approach to obstacles gives you the wisdom you need to be able to reach your goal. It not only sets you up for success – it sets you up to sustain your success. It's not a one-time success; rather success is the place you call home – the place where you are most comfortable – it lines up with your most deeply held beliefs – it's where you live and how you maintain your lifestyle.

The pursuit of a target brings to light areas that are demanding growth in our lives if we expect to make further progress. Challenges identify sabotaging beliefs, ineffective market positions and faulty systems.

Finding what works takes work. Don't despair! This is developing the true nature of wealth. It is in the development of your heart that you increase your ability to serve others in valuable ways they want to pay you for.

It is common that in the middle of implementing a plan, the situation demands more of you than you think you have.

What do these challenges look like?

They may come in the form of a difficult relationship. You will be tempted to emotionally check out, yell at, or rebuke someone for "ruining" your life and messing up your plans. Instead, choose the higher, more effective way. See that person as a gift-wrapped package sent into your life to make you better. View them as helping you increase your ability to connect and work with people who are not perfect.

Working with the mistakes and weaknesses of others without losing your peace and giving up your goal will further equip you with the tools and skills you so desperately need. You become better equipped to reach your destination.

The challenge may be bad economic times, weather problems or not getting the contract you worked so hard for.

Regardless of the difficulty, you know that what happens TO you is nothing compared to what happens IN you. There's nothing too difficult that comes to you that won't work FOR you. Challenges actually bow down and serve you by equipping you with skills and mindsets that are needed to reach the destination you made plans for.

Consider Rick Little's experience.[2]

Just after graduating from high school, Rick was in a very serious car accident. His car crashed into a tree and he broke his back. As he was at home recovering, he found his mother on the kitchen floor, overdosed on pills.

He felt like his whole life was crashing in around him and he was not adequately prepared to handle these difficult challenges. Out of his pain and out of the lessons learned from his hardships came a dream to equip high school students with the skills needed to become a success after they graduated.

He read a study of over one thousand 30 year old adults and they were asked if they felt their education had prepared them to succeed in life. Most said no; they were not prepared. They wished they had more training in relationship skills, handling conflicts, and financial management.

Rick traveled around the country and personally interviewed over two thousand students. To cut expenses, he lived in his car for 2 months.

He wrote grant after grant, requesting funding for his dream. As a matter of fact, he hired a grant writer and they wrote 155 grants – and 155 times, they were turned down.

In the pursuit of his dream, he spent all of his money and had to sell his car and all of his possessions. He found himself $32,000 in debt.

His grant writer was about to give up. He told Rick that he would help him write one more grant. If that did not work, he would have to find another job to support his family. This last grant was submitted to the Kellogg Foundation, asking for $55,000.

Two weeks later, Rick heard from the chairman of the foundation. The man told him that the trustees voted against granting him the $55,000 he had asked for.

Rick felt crushed. What was he going to do with his dream? Tears began to well up in his eyes. Before he could say anything, the chairman told Rick, "although we didn't vote for the $55,000 request, the trustees voted to grant you $130,000!"

Rejuvenated, Rick Little continued to pursue his dream. Since then, he raised over $100 million dollars and has reached over 30,000 schools in dozens of countries around the world.

He had a goal and he stayed focused on it. The obstacles and challenges didn't stop him, they simply made him more determined and better skilled to achieve his dream. By writing down his plan and relentlessly pursuing it despite the obstacles, his heart was developed with the skills needed to become the success he became.

An example in my life comes to mind.

Our organization, Redmond Leadership Institute, reaches, restores, and releases leaders to successfully lead their organizations.

As part of our work, we conduct Leaders' Outreaches in various countries. In the early stages of our organization, we were hosting our first conference designed to reach the business community in Bolivia.

My wife and I had poured heart and soul into this outreach. I had spent months working with the Bolivia team we had assembled. We made several trips to Santa Cruz and had gone into dozens of businesses, universities, churches and media centers to train the people and promote the business conference.

"Is this event worth the effort?" This was the question I was faced with by the Bolivian team we had assembled as I arrived to finish the preparations nine days before the event. Only 18 tickets were sold and we had spent or were soon to spend over $40,000.

Because it was our first big event and we hadn't invited business leaders and churches from the United States to help fund these outreaches at that time, we were covering the costs ourselves. We had a lot on the line.

Our team appeared to be overwhelmed and discouraged by the massive resistance they encountered. Even the best hopes saw that we would attract only a small group of business leaders. But God had other plans. . .

After much prayer and getting valuable input from our team, we reworked our marketing plan and launched it with a huge level of energy. From that point on, we gained enormous favor with the largest newspaper in the nation as well as the top two TV stations.

The lineup of speakers and I teamed up and we were filling the nation with hope on national TV – for five times longer than the program manager had planned! Our outstanding team set up countless other interviews, press coverage and TV spots throughout the week before the event. We worked day and night.

We continued to visit dozens of companies and I trained them in leadership, teamwork principles and how to motivate their employees. This generated a very positive response towards attending the event.

The night before the event, it was still uncertain how successful our efforts were. Even with the extensive and positive press coverage and training hundreds of executives and employees, some thought we would generate a maximum of 300 attendees. Many of us on the team thought otherwise. Our hearts were filled with faith and we knew God was at work.

As leaders, all of us, when we are in the middle of the pursuit of our dreams, will be challenged in the quest to obey His call. He told me that He was calling me to be obedient even in the face of certain failure. On the outside, it didn't look positive at all. In my heart, however, the Lord told me, "I'm in this and watch what I will do at this event."

If you trust God as your senior business partner, He will lead you to success. Sure enough, by 8:30am, the foyer was jammed with over 500 people and by the time the event started at 9am, over 600 business leaders crammed into the auditorium for the event!

We provided a seminar unlike they had ever experienced before.

As they raced to get their seats, the videos were playing, the lights were flashing, and the music was blaring. The atmosphere was filled with positive energy.

After each break, these business leaders poured back into the auditorium, hungry for more teaching that we delivered with powerful presentations and memory-sticking multimedia clips.

The most important part of the day was during our "bonus" session. I had my father-in-law, Bob Harrison lead this. As Bob artfully painted a picture of the need for spiritual success only available by making a decision for Jesus Christ as their Lord and Savior, hundreds of these leaders responded!

What would have happened if I didn't embrace those challenges as opportunities to count it all joy? What would have happened if I would have given up before reaping the tremendous harvest?

At the beginning of the plan, you are usually not equipped with all of the skills that are needed to reach your desired destination. Although you want to further develop your strengths and eliminate the negative effect of weaknesses, hardships help you in this development process.

Always remember, it is in the PURSUIT of our plans and goals that character, skills, and persistence is built into us through these challenges.

Always remember, it is in the PURSUIT of our plans and goals that character, skills, and persistence is built into us through these challenges. They work to prepare, equip and qualify us to reach our destination. What a joyful way of looking at difficulties!

This mindset and principle – that the development of your heart is the primary benefit of pursuing your dreams and goals – will give you a whole new attitude when you face challenges in achieving your plans. Remember, you are wired for success!

As you pursue your plan persistently, your heart becomes increasingly powerful. That is why Planning Principle 2 explains how to begin to plan in a way that brings enthusiasm, clarity and purpose . . .

Power Planning Principle 2:
Start with Your Heart

Most people start their planning and goal achieving with their head.

Let me share with you a recent experience of a dear friend.

He felt compelled to begin the planning process for his business and his personal life. He started the planning process in the traditional way by doing the following:

1. Revisited and clarified his vision, mission, values

2. Wrote his strategic plan which included listing the key goals to reach, key milestones to note if he was below, on, or above the plan's expectations, and doing a SWOT Analysis (listing Strengths, Weaknesses, Opportunities, and Threats).

3. Deliberated the tactical steps (specific Action Items including who owns the task, when will they complete it and who and what resources they need to accomplish the Action Item by the agreed upon date).

I recommend following these steps AFTER completing my planning system as they compliment each other. I have personally used systems developed by:

- Dr. Henry Migliore, *Strategic Planning and Management; Church and Ministry Strategic Planning; Strategic Planning for Healthcare Organizations*
- Jim Collins, *Beyond Entrepreneurship – Turning Your Business Into An Enduring Great Company*
- James Halcomb, *Courageous Leaders: Transforming Their World*

These are very important steps (outlined in the above books) in the planning process and should not be ignored.

However, after working through each of these points and completing his plan, my friend found that he was NOT excited about his plan. He felt frustrated, bored, and creatively flat with no motivation.

This was planning for his life – this was too vital to treat lightly!

His heart just was not into it and felt the whole process was a waste of time.

Then he called me. After working with him for 3 hours and walking him through this process, he was excited, focused and back in the saddle. He was ready to attack life with clarity and vigor.

The following pages explain the powerful approach that I brought him through.

Are you ready to involve your heart in this planning process?

Planning must start in your heart. There's immeasurable power in the heart – much more than what your mental capacities can provide.

In your heart is where you:

1. Connect with God.

He has a driving desire to communicate, walk with, and mentor you in a way that expands and fills you with ideas, capabilities, and plans that go way beyond what you could naturally do. It is from your heart that you hear His heart.

2. Exercise great faith.

Your heart is the place where all things are possible to you. It is from this inside world that you change the outside world. It is where your powerful Internal Success System is released to attract and accomplish anything that it strongly believes and is most deeply committed to.

3. Effectively connect with others.

Wealth is created primarily in our connections with others. I define "wealth" as "creation of value to effectively serve others" (this is covered in detail in my CD Seminar, *Wealth Manifesto – Releasing Your Unique Power to Create Wealth*).

Living and responding from our heart – especially in learning to connect and stay connected with others is one of the most powerful aspects of your unique greatness.

It is in the connection with others that you rescue, restore, and release the unique greatness in them. It is only by connecting your heart with God and others that you feel the significance and satisfaction that you are yearning for.

I've devoted a whole series to the power and advantage you have when living and leading from your heart. It is called *Leadership from the Heart* – for more information on this CD Seminar, please contact Redmond Leadership Institute.

When you start with your heart in the planning process, you will begin moving towards fulfilling your purpose with greater clarity and energy. The next chapter will explain how this unique approach will enable you to begin to live out one of the most significant yearning from your heart . . .

Power Planning Principle 3:
Focus on Freedom

Planning from your heart has one key focus. Let me explain.

I've asked a certain question to a number of groups that I have trained in many nations. Of those who own their own businesses, I ask, "Why did you get into business? Think way back to when you first decided to run your organization. What motivated you to make that decision?"

I have heard all kinds of answers to this question,

- to be my own boss
- make my own decisions
- earn more money
- train employees in the way I want to train them
- serve customers in the unique way that I want to serve them

After hearing hundreds of these responses from all over the world, I've come to realize there is one common denominator underlying all of them. What drives people to get into their own business or to run their own organization is one word.

That word is FREEDOM.

If you are a business owner, isn't this at least partially true with you? If you want to run the organization you're part of or someday start your own, what's driving that desire?

If you think deeply enough about it, you'll probably run into the same conclusion. You crave freedom. Freedom is what your heart is crying out for. Freedom to completely live and express your God-given greatness powerfully through your life.

Think of Jesus. What was His focus? He came to lead us into an abundant life. He came with the purpose to set the captives free. His focus was freedom – to set the powerful hearts of people free. His purpose was to release the power of your heart!

What was the mission of Jesus? He came to give us Freedom! As John wrote in his Gospel, Jesus said if you will continue in the word – if you will really begin to think and live the way I am leading you to – I will lead you to freedom. A few verses later, it says that whom the Son (that is, Jesus) sets free is free indeed! There is no question or debate about it. You are free!

If freedom was the focus of Jesus, should it also be our focus? Freedom should the focal point of all of our planning and goal achieving.

Most people get so busy living their lives they get pulled into the fray of everyday life. They work IN their business but not ON it. They forget that the desire for more freedom drove them to start their businesses in the first place.

The Power Planning system is pulling back and making sure that your life is "planned" around freedom.

All of our goals, plans and steps are subjugated to freedom. Does this step or plan or goal push me into the freedom that I am called to operate in? That is the question we must constantly ask ourselves as we work through our planning process.

In the material that follows, I will further define what freedom is and how to plan around the unique freedom that your destiny is demanding of you.

I was helping a guy grow his business from a few hundred thousand to several million dollars. After listening to his thoughts, desires, and concerns, I gave him a very dramatic thought to consider. Here's the thought:

Focus on freedom, not profitability.

His first response was, "I can't forget profitability. I have all kinds of bills to pay, a family to take care of, employees to pay . . . I have all kinds of commitments that I must keep. How can I forget about profitability?!!"

I did not tell him to forget about profitability; rather, I told him to make freedom his main focus.

What does freedom look like?

Freedom is living boldly from the power of your heart. It is breaking from the bondage of fears that suppress who you are and what you were created to contribute to the lives of others.

When you are free to do what you love, when you are free to do what you do best, when you are free to do the things that give you the biggest results, freedom will actually **increase** your profitability!

Although he was truly helping and serving people in his business, he was not operating with a sense of peace and freedom of which he was capable. The lack of peace and freedom was robbing him of the creativity needed to increase the profits that his business had the potential of producing.

So how do you gain this freedom and produce the wealth that your internal greatness is capable of producing? How do you transcend the relentless, daily demands that seem to block any hope for freedom?

Jesus addressed this very issue. Instead of absorbing all of your energies and attention seeking after how you are going to meet your needs, He directed you to seek first the kingdom of God.[3]

Where do you find the Kingdom of God? Jesus said the Kingdom of God is within you.[4]

Operating from the Kingdom of God is operating from a place of great power and abundance – instead of reacting with your head, you can creatively respond from the God-given, God-directed power in your heart!

What is the Kingdom of God? When we seek the kingdom of God, we are seeking righteousness, peace, and joy.[5]

These 3 internal qualities make up the foundation of the Kingdom of God. They are also some of the most commonly held definitions of true success by people all over the world, regardless of culture or religious persuasion.

They are also the three key foundation stones of the Wealth Creation Process that I teach in my *Creating Wealth God's Way* seminars. They are the stepping stones to enter into the freedom to most effectively release the unique greatness He put within you.

Here is a brief description of these 3 attributes:

1. Righteousness.

Bible teachers take dozens of hours to define righteousness and the essential role it plays in our success. For brevity's sake, I will paint a picture in your mind without sacrificing Biblical accuracy. Imagine a thick wire with connecting jacks on either end. One jack is plugged into the heart of God and the other is plugged into you. Righteousness is connecting God and all He is directly into you with no interference or anything blocking the connection. Righteousness results in having supercharged downloads coming from God's heart to yours. These downloads are filled with His thoughts and ways (which are so much better than ours[6]) of approaching your past, present and future.

As a result of these downloads, your heart is expanded by the huge and powerful plans He has for your life and business. See Him revealing (downloading) those plans to you as you spend time praying and communicating with Him.

What are the downloads? They include solutions to difficult problems, creative approaches to better serve your customers and create more value for them. With your intimate connection with Him, He stretches you beyond your current condition and abilities to enable you to make bold and powerful plans!

Righteousness means that your heart is made right with God; not because of what you have done but because of what you have received. Righteousness means that you have a powerful free-flowing connection with God. You are connected with the resources of heaven. It means that you can talk and interact directly with Him and receive His wisdom and thinking. He wants you to believe that ALL things are possible to you!

2. Peace.

With righteousness, your thoughts are transformed by His thoughts, making you better equipped and more powerful on the inside. Your plans are expanded by God's plans.
Peace then helps you take the next step. Peace removes the confusion and conflict you may have within and with God and it gives you tremendous clarity and confidence with which to make powerful choices.

Every great plan requires you to make tough decisions. With the peace of God, you can make those ongoing decisions confidently! I know of a man who began with hardly $50 to his name. As he prayed, he began to see the world around him differently. He saw opportunities in real estate that he never saw before and began buying and selling property. Before each purchase or sale, he connected with God (e.g., he prayed continually!) UNTIL he had peace in his heart about what to do.

He rarely rushed this vital process. He allowed the peace of God within him to have the final say and would not make a decision without it (he insisted that the peace of God rule or act as an umpire having the final say in his life![7]).

Over time, he became one of the largest property owners in Orange County, CA, and is now a billionaire!

3. Joy in the Holy Ghost.

Now for the third foundation stone in the Kingdom of God – joy in the Holy Ghost. We know that the joy of the Lord is our strength[8]. God's joy in us gives us strength to implement the plans we received by connecting with God in His righteousness. His joy in us enables us to take action on our decisions made in the peace of God.

We do not just make plans; we are busy taking action to **implement** the plans with extra strength and executive ability that the joy of the Lord provides!

When we understand how to make God-inspired plans from our heart, to make key decisions relating to the plan with God's peace ruling in our hearts and to implement them with tremendous strength that comes from the joy of the Lord, it gives us a huge advantage to implement our plans.

So many plan and live their life with such an intense focus on the destination that they lose their peace. Confusion and fear creeps in to rob from them the peace that is so necessary to make bold and confident decisions.

The kingdom of God instructs you to seek peace and even to pursue it. And with the peace of God ruling in your heart, you will begin to produce huge results. Those operating outside the kingdom of God forget about their connection with God and are implementing their plan in their own strength. As a result, they are burned out, disillusioned or have lost the intimate fellowship they once had with the Lord.

If this describes you in some way, today is a day you can turn that around!

These 3 things – righteousness, peace and joy are the keys to live a powerful life on this earth. They are the foundation stones for the wealth creation process and are also a necessary part in guiding you to live a life of freedom.

With your planning subjugated to solving for freedom to live from the greatness of your heart, the next logical step is to discover the desires of your heart . . .

Power Planning Principle 4:
Fire of Desire

The Planning Process – especially when you plan from your heart – uses clearly defined and deeply cherished desires as the key fuel to propel your plan forward.

There is tremendous power in desire. It is like the seed that begins an unlimited creative process. "Desire, like the atom, is explosive with creative force," stated Paul Buser.

As Napoleon Hill says, "the starting point of all achievement is desire. Weak desire brings weak results, just as a small amount of fire makes a small amount of heat. When your desires are strong enough you will appear to possess superhuman powers to achieve."

Here is a powerful question to ask in order to discover your true, heartfelt desire: What do you want? What do you really want?

I am not referring to percentage increases, key economic and financial measurements and all of the other "head" stuff. These are all very important and should be addressed in the planning process. But the first focus is your heart – what is your heart really crying out for?

To release your God-given greatness, you must have specific desires.

To release your God-given greatness, you must have specific desires. Many get so busy with their lives, they rarely take time to listen to their heart and know their desires. Or they have so many desires they don't tap the power that focused desires can bring. It's like what Thomas Fuller said, "If your desires be endless, your cares and fears will be so, too."

What is your desire? Take a moment to write it down so you can read it often.

Jesus excelled at providing solutions. Part of His secret was what He focused on. Before he helped others, He asked this question, "what do you want from me?"

And that is what He is asking you today. What do you really want?!!

So many are afraid of having or going after their desire. They may be afraid it is not God's will or their desires won't honor Him. Perhaps they are afraid of failing or being disappointed if it doesn't come to past.

We should always begin our planning process in the same way that King David of ancient Israel did. Before he made plans or decisions, he inquired of the Lord. He asked for God's insights and His plans. This is an effective pattern to follow.

Come to the Lord with a heart of surrender. Surrender any of your limited perspectives for His powerful, unlimited perspective. Staying in His presence builds you up, makes you stronger, and gives you a bigger or more effective plan. In His presence, ALL things are possible.

Planning is built on a strong foundation of faith. Yet sometimes our fear, though it may seem holy, can actually create a double-mindedness within us. Double-mindedness weakens our whole planning and goal achieving process. It creates an environment of instability. It's like the cross-eyed hunter trying to shoot his target. He sees two and misses both.

God lives and communes with you in your heart. He has made your heart good through the work of His son on the cross and the resurrection. Stay surrendered AND don't be afraid of the desires the come up from your heart during those times of prayer.

Are all desires good and Godly? Of course not! There are evil desires that create corruption.[9] Check your motives with each desire. Any desire that destroys or disrespects others and yourself is NOT a desire that comes from your heart.

Keep in mind that as His child, God has created within you a good heart and filled it with good desires. Desires that glorify Him, serve others and bring you into the abundant life He is calling you into.

That's why Jesus said, "Whatever you desire, when you pray, believe that you receive them and you will have them."[10]

The beginning of the powerful faith process – the start of getting your Internal Success System operating effectively is having a distinct and specific desire.

The word "de-sire" actually means "from the sire" or from the king. Your desires, especially when you seek to follow the Lord, are from your Heavenly Father.

Just recently, a business woman came to me after hearing some of these thoughts that I was sharing in a seminar. She said, "thank you, thank you thank you! I had so much doubt about this. I didn't know it was OK to have desires. I feel like you've awakened my heart with the freedom to desire once again!"

So what do YOU want?

Think big! Be creative in your imaginations. As one motivator said, "Don't go into something to test the waters, go into it to make waves." Whatever your desire, "decide that you want it more than you are afraid of it," encouraged Bill Cosby.

Please take a moment to write down your heart-felt desires on the Downloadable "Fire of Desire" Power Planning Tool that is available with the purchase of this book.

Assuming you've taken time to fill out the "Fire of Desire" Planning Chart, you know what you want. Although you've progressed way beyond most, just having desires is not enough. Your desires must be reinforced by a deep understanding of a planning concept rarely used. It is explained in the next chapter.

Power Planning Principle 5:
Plan Both Directions

Let's go back to my friend's story. He knew all of the "head" processes of planning but I could see his heart wasn't alive towards it. He felt stuck.

So I asked him, "if you were me sitting across from you, how would you advise yourself?"

He stated 3 things:

1. Identify what you want (your plan) and take steps towards fulfilling it. Even if they are small steps, identify specific steps to create motion towards implementing your plan.

2. Prioritize those steps. Some are more important than others. Some have to be done before you can begin others. Eliminate any steps that are not necessary. Keep your steps as clear and simple as you can.

3. Implement those steps – item by item. Take action until those steps are accomplished.

What he told me was profound. Identify, prioritize and implement specific steps.

When we take steps, what are we doing? "Steps" denote movement and direction.

When you step towards something, what else is happening? When you step TOWARDS something, you are always – at the same time - stepping away FROM something.

Here is where most miss it in planning (even planning experts in the biggest companies in the world). Most planners only focus on where they are going.

What they don't realize is that when they move TOWARDS something and they are also moving FROM something. They need to identify the goals they want to move towards AND be specific with what they don't want. In other words, what they want to move AWAY from.

Now before we go any further with this thought, I want to share with you one of the most powerful concepts in human motivation.

There are only two reasons why you or anybody else makes a decision or takes any action. These constitute the backbone of the whole body of motivational science. The whole basis of any action, decision, commitment, and movement in your life is based on one or both of these two factors.

First, we take action to gain a benefit – to move towards pleasure.

The second reason is we take action to avoid a loss – to move away from pain.

This is known as the Pain/Pleasure Principle. (A detailed discussion of this principle is included in my CD Seminar called *Leadership from the Heart*.)

If we can identify our desires – what we really want – and make abundantly clear the benefits and pleasure we'll get by moving towards that desire AND (this is important) we identify what we do NOT want – what we want to move away from and assign massive amounts of pain to what we want to move FROM, we will begin to see our desires come to pass.

This concept is SO powerful!

Since the Pain/Pleasure Principle affects our lives so dramatically, why not start your planning process the same way? Start with your heart and focus on freedom. Let freedom be the framework of all your planning and goals. Then identify your desires and be specific about what you are moving towards and what you are moving away from . . .

We can see the Pain/Pleasure Principle illustrated when the children of Israel came out of Egypt after 400 years of bondage.

They clearly saw the benefit of moving towards the Promised Land. However, they didn't associate or link enough pain to where they were coming from (referring to Egypt, the land of their slavery at that time). As they began to pursue their plan (moving towards the Promised Land), they "attracted" the resources they needed to reach their goal.

Because it was such a powerful plan, it also attracted obstacles and hardships. These challenges were meant to strengthen their hearts and equip them to be able to reach their destination of the Promised Land. Since they didn't link enough pain and loss to where they were moving from, they turned back to the slavery of the past instead of pressing on "towards" their promised land.

When they were under pressure, instead of becoming stronger and more determined, their challenging experiences became bigger than their goal.

Know that you will always win when what you learn from your experiences is bigger than the pain of the experience. Learning is an essential aspect of creating wealth God's way. What's the opposite of learning? Blaming. One goes inward to your place of strength and makes adjustments accordingly. The other goes outward assigning reasons and excuses for not taking personal responsibility.

> **You will always win when what you learn from your experiences is bigger than the pain of the experience.**

All plans require adjustments along the way. In fact, Robert Allen says you may find your place of success lies perpendicular to your original plan.[11] Learning denotes growing, adapting and adjusting. When you focus on learning instead of blaming, you set the stage to more readily and effectively adjust to optimize your results.

The Israelites were looking on the outside instead of the beautiful work going on inside their hearts. The hardships (which they refused to view as learning opportunities – instead they chose to blame and complain) appeared bigger than the reward of reaching their goal. After 40 years of wandering in the wilderness, they died in defeat, never reaching their promised land.

They robbed themselves of the dignity they wanted in having their own nation and land. Because they gave up in their faith (what they saw on the inside) to obtain their goal, they traded their potential greatness for a life of blaming and complaining . . . except for 2 men.

Joshua and Caleb approached their experience just the opposite of the rest. They became bigger than their challenges because they made it clear in their thinking where they were headed to and where they were headed from. They were convinced that they were "well able" to achieve the plan of conquering their promised land.

They linked tremendous pleasure and fulfillment to achieving their goal. They also associated unbearable pain to remaining a slave in Egypt or a wanderer in the desert.

What did their future look like? They went forward and conquered.

Are you ready to enter your "promised land?"

Summary of Key Points So Far

Since we learn and are changed by repetition, let's take a moment to review the key points so far.

1.   Power of Your Beliefs. Who are you and what are your capacities? You create your reality with your most deeply held beliefs. Whatever you believe begins to show up in your life in some way. Why not focus on who you really are with all of your strengths and creative abilities?!!

2.   Planning and goal achieving plays such an important role in your life. This positive process is a concrete way to begin to release the creative abilities of your heart. You can begin reigning in life as a king rather than living as a slave to the circumstances of life.

3.   Power Planning Principle 1: The Power is in the Pursuit. The Pursuit of your plan sets in motion the primary benefit of planning – that is, developing your heart to see, respond and create with increasing effectiveness. Whether the experience is positive or negative, you make it your teacher to further equip and release the greatness of your heart.

4.   Power Planning Principle 2: Start with Your Heart. The planning process – the journey to achieve – is actually a journey to develop your heart. Living and planning from the power of your heart will better enable you to reach your destination.

5.   Power Planning Principle 3: Focus on Freedom. Building your plan around giving you more freedom to do the things you are called and love to do will infuse added strength, energy and needed perseverance when you are tempted to give up.

6.   Power Planning Principle 4: Fire of Desire. You have to give yourself a target to direct your energies and attention towards. Desires are the raw material of faith – your ability to create your

future NOW. That is why it is so important to be very specific with your desires. You have to be deliberate in knowing and writing down your desires. What do you really want?

7.   Power Planning Principle 5: Plan Both Directions. When you write your desires and set up key targets to reach in your plan, they should describe two directions – where you are moving towards and where you are moving from.

In this planning process, attach huge amounts of pleasure to the "towards" direction. Make the reasons and benefits of achieving the plan extremely clear. Make it so clear that it excites and stirs you and fills you with joy! Make your plan so clear, you begin to see, feel, touch, taste, and hear the enjoyment of that plan even BEFORE it actually comes to pass!

Questions open your imagination and release creativity.

Also clearly identify what and where you are moving from. You are associating huge amounts of pain and loss and discomfort to the past and current situation.

Make it clear how dangerous it is to be satisfied with the past or current results. See them robbing you of reaching your destination. Specify the old, ineffective way of thinking, reacting, blaming, and doing that you are moving away from.

Power Planning Principle 6:
Ask the Right Questions

Now it is time to begin implementing the concepts shared so far.

We discovered the more powerful way to the planning and goal achieving process does not begin in your head – it begins in your heart.

Focus on tapping the power of your heart because that is the place where you connect with God and where your thoughts and plans are expanded by His perspective. You can then walk in more boldness and confidence because of your ongoing interaction with Him.

Your heart is also the place where you exercise great faith and the outside world begins to conform and align to the vision and plan you have deeply committed to within your heart.

It is also the place where you connect with the hearts of others to positively impact their lives. Satisfaction and significance fills your life when you release the unique greatness in your heart to enrich and help others.

All of your goals and plans should be made in the framework of freedom. Each step of the plan should take you further in your walk towards total freedom to do and be what you were created for.

With a focus on freedom, know that you have to be specific in your desires – in what you really want. Desire is the starting point of planning with great faith, power and results.

So what are the specifics to discover and plan for the unique freedom and desires that your heart wants to pursue?

A well thought out plan specifies both what you want and what you don't want. Clearly identify what you are moving towards and link or associate enormous pleasure and benefits to those steps in your plan.

Then make a list of what you are moving away from and link tremendous pain and loss to each of those items.

Using the "Define Your Freedom" Power Planning Tool provided to you from my website, invest time answering these strategic questions.

There is tremendous power in asking the right questions.

Questions open your imagination and release creativity. They create a vacuum in your heart that must be filled. Your mind and heart are designed to seek out and find answers to the questions you ask.

Higher quality questions will produce higher quality results in your life. In other words, ask better questions and you'll get better answers.

The questions that follow will remove the clutter of fleeting, negative thoughts and will focus your mind and heart on the most important things in your life.

7 Powerful "Towards" Questions

1. **What would you do if you knew that you knew you couldn't or wouldn't fail?**

This question gives you permission to dream big! Imagine that you have no limitations; you could do whatever you wanted to do. What would that be? What would that look like?

This question strips the straightjacket of limiting beliefs off of your thinking and allows you to see yourself doing and becoming things that your thinking hasn't allowed you to see before.

If you knew you couldn't fail regardless of the circumstances that come your way, what would you begin to pursue?

You'll never be defeated if what you learn from the experience is greater than the pain of the experience. EVERY experience is designed to teach you something greater than the pain or pleasure that may be attached to it.

See yourself taking any experience – positive or negative – and making it bow down to serve your plans, goals and dreams. See them developing, stretching and equipping your heart to accomplish the great things your heart is yearning to be released to do. If you think about it clearly enough, this question will destroy a number of fears that are trying to imprison you from dreaming and planning big.

The fear of failure will try to keep you from making some bold and tough decisions that your plan is requiring you to make and take action on. Making choices is the essential aspect of reigning in life as a king.

The fear of failure is closely related to the fear of dealing with and resolving issues that will derail your pursuit of your goals. What decisions or steps have you been putting off that TODAY you can decide and take action on that will move you towards accomplishing your dream?

As you consider these thoughts, write down what your life would look like if you began to live in the freedom of an unlimited mindset. Write whatever comes to your mind without worrying about how well it is written at this time.

2.   **What is it that you really want in every part of your life?**

If you had everything that you could possibly want, what would you have?

If you could design your ideal lifestyle, what would it look like?

If you could design your ideal career, what would it be?

See yourself living out in the present tense. What are you doing? Who is working with you and how are you helping them and them helping you? Take a moment to visualize this now.

Who are your customers? Who is receiving the benefit from your product or service and what are they saying about how their lives were helped and improved by the value you provided them?

Take time to capture whatever comes to your thoughts at this time.

3.   **What do you produce or create that others see as valuable? Another way of asking this is what are you great at creating?**

Here's a concept I want you to think about for a moment: Focus on creating value, not pursuing money. Who's the leader and who's the follower? Why pursue that which is designed to be a follower?

Although I cover the Wealth Creation Process in more detail with "Wealth ManifestoTM – Tapping Your Unique Power to Create Wealth," let me define why the word "value" is so important.

Most people think that wealth is money. I define wealth differently. Wealth is more than just the generation of money or the accumulation of goods. Wealth is the creation of value. It's the ability to produce something of value or importance for others.

Deuteronomy 8:18 reveals a special gift He gave His people. It is the "power to create wealth."

I define and expand this phrase first by defining the word "power." What is the power in this context? The power is the ingredients and mixing pot for creating value – for creating wealth.

That power is actually the Holy Spirit working with your natural and spiritual gifts and skills, working with your character and integrity, and the wisdom you've gleaned from your experiences, successes, failures, and hard work to get or create or produce something valuable with which to serve others.

Wealth creation is the process of creating and delivering something of value to someone else. This unique planning process is really a focus on improving your ability to create value – to produce more wealth in your life.

To live an abundant life in the Kingdom of God, the focus is not on making money but in creating wealth. Creating products and services that are so valuable, others want to exchange something of value with you to get it. It's really a value exchange between two or more people. Your value increases when you are focused on serving other people with your unique God-given abilities.
So focus on creating value, not generating money.

Wealth is a creation of God; money is a creation of man.

So is money bad? Of course not! Money simply takes on the nature of the person holding it. When you employ money for noble causes, it is a wonderful tool to enjoy! I help organizations and individuals create large amounts of profit and money. The question remains, what are you pursuing? Whatever you pursue, you serve in some way.

Money is generated by creating value. It is a by-product of the main thing you are to focus on. Money follows the creation of value.

When money leads (becomes the driving, controlling factor), it is called Mammon. When Mammon is in operation, corruption emerges in some way.

Our focus is wrong when we are chasing or getting money instead of using our unique God-given greatness to create value.

Money is a bad leader but a great follower. What does money follow? It follows the creation of wealth – it follows value. Value attracts money; the lack of perceived value repels it.

Money is a bad leader but a great follower.

What is value? Value is created by implementing great ideas and strategies, developing reliable character and integrity, being diligent and becoming trustworthy to others, using your wisdom, and coming up with solutions to difficult problems. These are all products of your heart being fully alive!

4. What do you love to do?

This is my favorite question.

Doing what you love to do will improve in your life. In other words, when you are doing what you love to do, that thing that you love doing will get better. It will improve.

This is part of the power of freedom. Giving yourself freedom to do what you love to do will cause you to become better at it which will cause you to love it more which will cause you to get even better at it – and so on. Do you get the picture?

Giving yourself this freedom feeds on itself. The more you do it, the more wealth and value you will create.

Think back to when you were in school. Perhaps you are in school now (always be a student!). Think of the classes that you absolutely loved. How did you do in those classes? Chances are you did very well. You probably did your homework, diligently studied and applied yourself. Learning was fun!

What about that class that you didn't like? Or even hated? You were bored. You didn't see how the subject material applied to your life now and in the future. How well did you do? If there's a class you didn't score well in, it was probably this class.

If you do those things you love to do, you will get better at doing those things. So. . . what do you love to do?

You may be in a job or activity that you DON'T love. So, what do you do? In some rare cases, you are to leave immediately – as it says in the Monopoly Game, do not pass Go, do not collect $200 (but instead of going to jail, you are getting out!).

In most cases, the problem is how we are looking at what we are doing. As Stephen Covey said – the way we see the problem IS the problem.[12]

There is a way to "count it ALL joy" even in this situation. Many times, you lose your joy when you don't feel you have any choice or options in the situation. But the truth is, you ALWAYS have a choice. So how does that apply to the topic at hand?

There's a concept I call "transference." It is a process where you take your strengths, what you love to do and you apply them or "transfer them" to your current situation in some way.

I was talking to my brother John recently. He's a very accomplished electrical engineer with years of experience in the telecommunications industry. When I asked him about his job, his facial expression, tone and words told me he's doing something that he doesn't love to do. At least on the surface.

I asked him what he really loves to do. John loves to coach soccer but he quickly said, "but coaching soccer can't feed my family."

That's when I talked to him about "transference." I asked him to be specific in finding out exactly what it is about coaching soccer that he loves. He mentioned he loves the interaction, watching the kids grow and develop, he loves teaching and instructing.

Then I asked him, "How can you "transfer" the aspects of what you love with soccer to your current job or industry?

Using your technical knowledge and great communication skills you can get into training, consulting, analyzing weak strategies or routing issues and replacing it with better, more optimal ones."

It's important to know that you are not stuck where you are at. You always have options and choices. You can start your own business, change jobs or industries. Or you can choose to bloom where you are currently planted by utilizing the concept of transference.

Lasting and satisfying growth comes by taking thousands of little steps. Don't despise what may appear to be little steps you are taking. Little steps lead to big steps. As you are faithful in the little, you will grow in your responsibility, skills, and influence. Many skip necessary development areas because they jump around from one job or idea to another so frequently they rob themselves of dealing with crucial issues that the "faithful in the little" process provides them.

Here are some other ways of asking the "love" question . . .

What would you do even if you didn't get paid?

Another related question is: What gives you energy?

Energy . . . it seems to be a limited resource. If this is true with you, please consider this. Energy drain is not due to output as much as it due to these 3 things:

1. It is due to unfulfilled expectations.

2. It is due to NOT tapping the power of your heart or releasing your unique greatness into your key relationships and work.

3. It happens when you do not see purpose in what you do.

What kind of work creates great meaning for you?

After graduating from college and working for a senator in Washington, D.C. for a number of months, I began my professional career at PriceWaterhouse Coopers as a CPA auditing companies. Day in and day out, I found myself ticking and tying out numbers, writing memos and interacting with executives who were not always excited to see me.

The job doesn't make the man; rather, the man makes the job!

One day I asked myself, "What am I doing here? I feel like I am wasting my life!"

But here is another important thought to consider: The job doesn't make the man; rather, the man makes the job!

After thinking about my situation and going to the Lord in prayer about it, I pulled back a few steps from my current perspective. I began to see how what I was doing on a daily basis was tied to my larger purpose!

This was incredible training for the dream I had of going around the world waking up the greatness in people, reaching and developing leaders at all levels – top executives, pastors, and government and university leaders.

I am now living my dream.

It was important that I did not despise the work early in my career. I tied it into my purpose and it propelled me to a higher level of excellence. As a matter of fact, I remember moving from the bottom third of my peer group to one of the top 2 performers in less than one year. This happened after I tied my daily, seemingly menial tasks to my life purpose.

When you do what you love to do, what you do will improve!

Another way of asking the "love" question is: What makes my heart sing – what makes it come alive?

Here is one of my favorite quotes: "Don't ask what the world needs, ask what makes your heart come alive, for what the world needs is your heart fully alive!"[13]

Doing things with your heart fully alive will help the people attached to your life in significant and meaningful ways. It will give you more satisfaction than trying to chase after money and position.

If money and position is your focus, you will be distracted and unfulfilled. If freedom and living life with your whole heart fully alive is your focus, I believe the money and position and honor – or whatever you desire – those things the world seeks after – they will come to you in abundance! (For a more thorough explanation of money and the wealth creation process, check out my CD Seminar called *Wealth Manifesto – Releasing Your Unique Power to Create Wealth*.)

And I am not saying these things are bad. However, when you focus on freedom, focusing on making your heart fully alive, focusing on what you love to do, those things will come to you. They respond to the value you create. It is not a matter of pouring all of your energy into chasing after them.

All of these "other" things (such as money, influence, possessions) will follow the releasing of your unique greatness to create wealth and value for others.

5. What do you do that gives you the biggest results?

What relationships, types of people, customers, and friends give you the biggest results? (Biggest results are measured not only by the benefits you receive, but also by how much of your unique greatness they utilize and celebrate.)

A distracting deception is to get focused on spending 80% of your time on people and activities that only produces 20% of the results. Many of us know this as the 80/20 Pareto's Principle.

Time Allocation. This is a great time in your life to take inventory of how you spend your time and who you spend it with. There are times when I have kept detailed notes of how, where and with whom I spend my time for a couple weeks in a row. This keeps me accountable for how I spend my time. Try this for yourself and see what you discover.

Co-workers. Consider evaluating your relationships with co-workers. Some waste your time and there is very little "value exchange" between you for the time spent. This doesn't give you a license to be rude but it should give you a greater awareness and help you select who you deliberately want to invest your time and wisdom with.

Mentors/Mentorees. In a work environment, I always sought to find a mentor and to be a mentor. This habit has produced huge dividends in my life. It keeps me living from the power of my heart.

Customers. Consider reviewing a list of your customers. Spend more time nurturing a relationship with those customers who are the most profitable. With prospective clients, don't waste time continuing to call on unresponsive prospects.

Chances are you close more than 50% of your sales on 3 or less calls. So spend your time pursuing those potential customers who are most interested in talking to you. Is it really worth your investment calling 8 and 10 and 12 times on those leads that keep giving you excuses on why they can't meet with you? Drop them and move on to new prospects!

Friends. What about your friends? Consider the following exercise . . .

Circles of Influence. Write the word "me" in the middle of a page and drawing several enlarging circles around it. Each of these circles represents how much you focus on developing your relationships.

The circle closest to "me" on the page includes people you have the biggest heart connection with. These are the people you invest the most time, energy and creativity towards (and receive from) because of the value you exchange with one another.

The next circle may be those you are supervising. The circle beyond that may be people who you know but really don't contribute that much to your life or are not receptive to your wisdom and counsel. Write the names of people you know in the appropriate circle.

With the people in the inner circles – whether they are relatives, friends or customers – there should be a healthy and equal exchange between you and those people.

Leaders are deliberate, especially with the people they interact with. Consider making a list of who these people are (don't just think about it, make a specific list!).

Those circles further out from the center are people you invest less of yourself into. Be careful with the use of your time. If you spend your time only with people in the outer circles, it will flatten you and you will lose the power of living from your heart.

These are some great tips for managing your professional and personal life. They will also help you define your unique freedom and desires. When you identify those relationships and activities that give you the biggest results, you'll find clues to what your heart was designed to do and who to do it with.

6. **From your perspective, what breaks the heart of God – what causes Him to grieve and weep?**

This question may sound negative at first but it is really a "moving towards" question.

He put unique abilities and desires within you. He wants you to use them to help others. How does He want you to use your strength (abilities and desires) to create value in the lives of those you are called to help?

You see, your leadership is drawn to chaos. The purpose of your leadership is to bring lasting order to that chaos in the same way God created order out of chaos in the first chapter of Genesis.

Think about conversations with friends, articles in the newspaper or reports on the news station. What are you frustrated or angry about? Many times, your greatness is tied to that chaotic situation. Instead of getting mad and just talking about it, what can you begin to do to bring healing, strength, understanding – and ultimately, order to that chaos?

I have asked many of those I have mentored over the years, "are frustrations and disappointments your friends or foes?" Allow them to be friends who wake up your heart and identify your deepest desires.

7. **What do I do, that when I am doing it, I feel the closeness and presence of God without effort?**

Another way of asking this is: What does God take pleasure in watching me do?

I believe God loves to see you do what you love to do. It's not just some spiritual activity that you do at your church. God loves to see you develop and use the gifts that He breathed into you.

I believe God is involved with you when you are doing what you love to do.

A great example of this is my dad. He was a brilliant man with a doctor's degree in chemical engineering. When he gave his life to God; he wanted to show God how much he loved Him.

A common thought at that time was if you really loved God, you had to quit your job and go into the ministry on a full-time basis. People then didn't realize that your ministry consists of doing what God called them to do, whether it was designing, building, cleaning or teaching.

In the area of your gifting and expertise, God is involved, living in you and through you.

For years, my father would work in the ministry. He was miserable. Then he would go back into the chemical engineering field, running factories, developing new products, and cleaning up toxic waste sites. When he did that, he was happy again. He loved what he was doing!

Then he would go back into ministry work and again, he would become miserable. Eventually, he would get back into engineering work and he was happy.

Finally, during a time of devotion and study, my dad sensed the presence of the Lord. He heard the Lord speak in his heart and here is what he heard Him say, "Bill Redmond, I want you to know something. I love to be an engineer and I love to be an engineer through you!"

God loves to be who He is through you – He loves to live His life in you and through you when you are working with all your heart to serve the people around you.

So as you discover what your heart loves to do, know that God will be right there close to you. Don't despise what you love. Just be sure that what you love to do respects others and helps your community. Set your heart free! Give yourself freedom to chase after it with all of your heart.

"Bill Redmond, I want you to know something. I love to be an engineer and I love to be an engineer through you!"

By discovering what you love to do and are great at doing, doing what people want and need and will pay you in some way to get, your heart's unique freedom and desires will begin to emerge. Be sure to "chart" this discovery process by writing down all of your thoughts in the "Define Your Freedom" Power Planning Tool available from my website!

5 Clarifying "From" Questions

Start identifying "what to move away from" by simply asking and answering just the opposite of the "Towards" questions. Here are some additional "moving from" questions:

1. **What habits, thought patterns, actions or relationships are you allowing to rob you of dreaming and planning big?**

What is keeping you from going after that big dream that burns in your heart?

What is keeping you from dropping your limited, defeated thinking and moving into unlimited thinking?

The conditions outside of you do not determine your destiny. What determines who you become and where you go in life are the conditions on the inside of you – in your heart and mind.

2. **What do you really NOT want in your life that you are currently tolerating?**

You cannot complain about what you permit. So what are you currently permitting that you need to say, "no more!!"?

Pay attention to what you complain about. It will reveal either something you need to address and resolve or change your perspective about how you are looking at it.

What would you no longer be doing if your life were perfect in every respect? What would those things be?

3. **What do you hate to do?**

Please don't be afraid of answering this question. What do you hate to do? Write down what comes to mind. This cannot be overemphasized. It is so important to write down your responses.

There is one word of caution with this question. If what you hate has to do with another person, most of the time it is a "heart development" opportunity.

When dealing with others, an effective leader always goes inward and makes demands in his heart BEFORE he goes outward to deal with the issues in the other person's life.

This is a great question for having your heart revealed. What you hate should line up with God's heart. It should not deter you from celebrating the dignity of others or keep you from fulfilling your commitments.

For instance, if you hate spending time with your spouse or kids, then your perspective and approach will need to change. Your emphasis in these cases should be going inward, focusing on changing yourself, before going outward trying to change others so you will accept them.

Freedom ALWAYS comes with responsibility. This is not a bad word. Kings love responsibility. Those people who walk in freedom love responsibility. Those who reign in life, reign by taking responsibility.

People who act like slaves and paupers don't take responsibility. Instead, they run from truly taking personal responsibility. Their first response is always going outward to accuse and blame others before dealing with the issues in their own heart.

4. What drains you?

In other words, what activities are you involved in that doesn't give you energy and excitement?

This is another question to be careful with. It is important not to mistake an obstacle that your goal or plan has attracted for the thing that drains you. Deal with the obstacle in a way that expands and further equips you.

Challenges are things you are to "count it all joy." Remember what joy does for you? It gives you strength and energy. It gives you a wider viewpoint to see opportunities instead of just problems and limitations. When challenges come because you are implementing your goals, they can actually give you joy because they are making you stronger and more capable on the inside.

But don't be afraid of writing down those things that drain you because, many times, it will reveal what your heart is really trying to say.

5. **What activities and relationships create the smallest results for the time, concentration and energy exerted?**

Think back on the 80/20 principle that we covered earlier. It is important not only to identify these things but to also write them down. Make them visible and attach pain, loss, waste of time and resources with these items. Look at them like poison to avoid!

One of my favorite business authors, Jim Collins, wrote a book called Good to Great. This book is a study of a handful of companies that were average in their performance compared to their competitors in their industry. Each of these companies rose from being average to being the top leaders with their overall performance. What makes them unique is they were also able to sustain that top position for at least 15 years.

One of the secrets to their success was that each one of these companies had what Jim Collins calls "Level 5" leaders as the chief executive officer. They were chiefly responsible for leading their companies to the top position in the industry and keeping them there.

These "Level 5" leaders possessed both extreme humility and extreme commitment to their organizations. It wasn't about them. It was about serving their organizations and serving the employees and customers in their organizations.

Stop Doing It! Among other qualities, each of these great leaders not only maintained a "to do" list but all had a "Stop Doing" List. It was a list that reminded them of what activities and time-wasters they were going to deliberately avoid doing.

Failure is the result of not knowing what to do; success is the result of knowing what NOT to do.

What's on YOUR "stop doing" list? What is robbing you from creating value and from getting huge results? It may be a preoccupation with emails and text messages, reading reports and articles that don't really help your decision-making process. It may be watching too much TV or having meaningless conversations that don't stir the greatness in the hearts of the people you are interacting with.

What items are on your "stop doing" list? I challenge you to begin today by writing down a list of things that you are going to move from. Put a stop to those things that are distracting you from activities that give you the biggest results.

Responding with the powerful, 2-letter word will make you free. It will set your heart free to do those things that you love to do and keep you from doing those things that you should no longer be tolerating.

That word is "no"! What activities are you to say "no" to?

What are you tolerating in your life that you must say "no!" to?!! "No" is a very powerful word. It is the key to staying focused. Focus is the key to harnessing energy into a certain spot and getting the most important tasks done.

Saying "yes" too many times is going to dilute your energy, focus and overall efforts.

Leaders live deliberately. They know that low-payoff, meaningless activities will fill up their schedule unless they are ruthless in focusing on their priorities.

Busy people prioritize their schedules. Highly productive people schedule their priorities.

How about you? Say "no" to those activities that are robbing you from expressing your greatness!

Busy people prioritize their schedules. Highly productive people schedule their priorities. Although these 2 approaches sound similar, they produce massively different results!

This principle is best illustrated by the professor who started his class by filling up a large glass jar with 5 big rocks.

After filling the jar with these rocks, he asked the class, "is this jar full?" They responded, "of course it is."

Without saying a word, the professor picked up a bucket of gravel and poured it into the jar. The gravel filled in the spaces between the big rocks all the way up to the top of the jar.

He asked the class again, "is this jar full?" Those who were paying attention thought it was full but knew the professor was up to something. They said, "no, it is not full." "You're right, very good," the professor said.

Then he picked up a bucket of sand and filled the jar to the top once again. "Is it full now?" The class said, "We think so but probably not." "You're starting to catch on class," the professor said. He then picked up a bucket of water and filled up the jar to the top once again. The professor then said, "now this jar is full."

Then he asked, "what is the lesson in this illustration?" Most of the responses from the students were along the lines of "if you organize your time right, you can cram much more into your schedule."

Our mindset is to increase our busyness but not necessarily our productivity. There is a huge difference between these two concepts. Leaders deliberately schedule their priorities.

The professor then asked, "if I put the gravel, sand and water in first, how many of these big rocks do you think we could cram into this jar without breaking it?"

"Maybe one or two if we really work with it," the students responded.

If you try to cram all 5 big rocks into the jar AFTER filling it with the gravel, sand and water, you will end up breaking the jar. The same thing can happen in your life. If you try to get to the "big rock" activities AFTER doing the easier gravel, sand, and water activities, you will rarely accomplish the most important goals in your life.

So what is the lesson here? It's not about activity; it is about priorities.

If you don't put the big rocks in FIRST, you probably won't get to the big rocks. The big rocks are the most important results-getting activities. That's why you have to do more than just prioritize your schedule. You have to schedule your "big rock" items. You have to write them into your schedule first as the most important items to focus on. Then put all of the gravel, sand and water activities further down your schedule if you even schedule them at all.

What are your big rock items for today or this week? What are your big rock items for this month? How about for this year? As you identify these most important priorities and focus on implementing them, you will begin moving towards your freedom. You will begin to live with your heart fully alive.

The clearer and more intense your responses are to these questions, the more effectively you will tap your heart and move into your freedom. This will create a more solid launching pad to take decisive, powerful action in writing and implementing your plan.

You may have questions of your own. I encourage you add these to the list. In any case, get the ball rolling and begin to answer the questions mentioned here (use the Define Your Freedom Power Planning Tool provided online).

Begin to apply yourself to what you are hearing now, become a person of action.

There is so much in the planning process that can be derailed. One of the most important planning principles that stabilizes the process is explained in the next chapter . . .

Power Planning Principle 7:
Prayer in the Planning Process

As you answer the "Moving Towards" and "Moving From" questions, it is a great time to invite the Holy Spirit to interact with you.

Prayer is ESSENTIAL in planning process.

Proverbs 16:1, 3 are pivotal scriptures that frame the proper perspective on planning. "We can make our own plans, but the LORD gives the right answer. Commit your actions to the LORD, and your plans will succeed."

The key is knowing the Lord intimately enough to know how and when He gives us the "right answers."

There is a difference between casually knowing someone who is really successful versus being directly mentored by them. Perhaps there is a leader in your life that you really respect and want to be mentored by them.

If you only know that super successful person from a distance and do not interact with him, you will only know ABOUT him and the success principles that he mastered. Without the close, ongoing mentoring interaction, you'll be limited in mastering and applying the success principles into your life.

The same thing applies in your relationship with God. You can know of Him but not be changed by Him without those times of intimate prayer and seeking His wisdom.

God is someone who helps to make people successful. He is a master of success and of the wealth creation process. Remember, He is the one who taught the Jewish people to be successful!

It is essential to spend time really getting to know Him. This comes by speaking to Him and especially by listening to Him. As you do this, He will fill your heart with wisdom.

There's a story about a young man and very wise teacher. The young man rushed up with his eyes opened wide, "Master, can you impart more wisdom into my life?!"

"Sure, I will do so as we sit together at this table. Would you like some tea?" the master asked as he picked up the teapot.

"Yes but when are you going to teach me? I want to hear more of your wisdom!" the young man said. He could hardly sit still in his chair.

The old man began pouring tea into the young man's cup. Halfway. Then up to the top. He continued to pour tea into the cup even though it was overflowing onto the table.

"Master, master, please stop pouring! My cup is full; it can't hold any more tea!" the young man exclaimed.

"So it is with you mind, my young disciple. It is so busy and over-flowing with thoughts that you don't have room for any new thoughts," the wise master explained. "To receive wisdom, new insights and perspectives you must quiet your mind. Empty your cup, if you will, so you can make way for new ways of thinking."

So it is with your relationship with the wisest Master. He longs to impart wisdom into your life to help bring you to your wealthy place. Quiet your mind and open your heart as you communicate with Him.

In fact, prayer is more listening than speaking.

You will be changed in a very positive way by moving into a close relationship with Him. He may speak to you directly in your heart, through the Bible, other anointed books or speakers, or it may be through the inner circle of your friends.

In any case, the more you communicate and interact with God, the bigger and more confident you will become on the inside and the more effective your plan will be.

You are now ready to implement the last Planning Principle . . .

Power Planning Principle 8:
Align and Reinforce Your Freedom

The last step of the "Power Planning" Process is to align and reinforce your inside and outside world to move toward freedom.

Inside World

Let's begin with your inside world. What does this involve?

Be on guard with what you think, see and hear. Why is this so important? Because whatever you focus on will begin to show up in someway in your life.

That's why it's so important to feed your heart with nutritious food. As Zig Zigler says, "your output is determined by your input."

Here are some ideas for feeding your heart that have worked well for me.

1. Every day, I read the Bible.

My mother always told me the Bible is God's love letter written especially and personally to each one of us. I encourage you to read it like that.

Some of the greatest leaders in history read their Bible as their main source of guidance and strength. Allow the Bible to provide you guidance in your decision-making.

The Bible is going to help you make better choices. The choices we make are what determine the results in our lives. Choices are how you reign and become successful in life. I refer to the Bible as "The Book of Choices." It is going to help you make the right choices and the right choices are going to produce the right results in your life.

To go a step further with your time with the Bible, I encourage you to set time aside to thinking about key verses and chapters.

Meditating over the scriptures is one of the most productive uses of my time. It is when the "renewal of my mind" really begins. As I mull and say to myself over and over various truths, they begin to replace old thought patterns with positive, life-giving neural networks. It affects how I think, see, feel and act.

For example, just recently I woke up early and began to think about Proverbs 3:5. For forty-five minutes, I meditated intensely on that one verse. I thought about each word and phrase and began to see myself acting out trusting the in the Lord. What does it mean to trust? Being in the Lord? Lord means being boss – how can I have the Lord act as my boss? Over and over I thought of various aspects of this verse.

It is through self talk that we enable or disable our creative abilities.

What happened? Amazingly, my trust towards the Lord increased to the point it affected my emotional state. I carried myself with more confidence. Anxiety was replaced with an unflappable peacc.

Read the Word to give you fuel to meditate. Meditation is a way of directing your self talk. It is through self talk (what we say to ourselves about ourselves – both consciously and subconsciously) that we enable or disable our creative abilities. Through the meditation of the Word, that power is created.

2. **Along with the Bible, read other great books and listen to inspirational recordings as often as possible.**

By taking a few hours to read and listen to great authors, your heart will be expanded by the thoughts and concepts they worked hard all of their lives to develop. It speeds your learning process and makes your heart bigger and stronger.

3. **Another way to feed your heart is writing down what comes to mind during your time of prayer and reading the Bible and other great books.**

Whenever you are inspired by what you read or hear, write down the thought that comes to your mind during that time. Many great thoughts come and go and will soon be forgotten if you don't write them down the moment they come to you. Consider keeping an "Inspiration and Ideas" Journal at your side when you are reading and praying.

4. **Have "heart to heart" talks with trusted friends, mentors and "mentorees" as frequently as you can.**

As you open up your heart and talk about what is most important to you, what is in your heart will be unlocked and revealed – they will become clearer and easier to make plans and take action on in your life.

5. **Finally, as you write your plans and goals, consider reading them out loud at the start and end of your day.**

Hear yourself saying what you are moving towards and what you are moving away from. There is tremendous power in the spoken word – especially if it is YOU doing the speaking!

When you do this every day, it will make your plan more powerful and easier to accomplish. It will strengthen your belief system, clarify the direction you are headed and give you more power to make better choices.

It is great to declare your goals on a daily basis. It is equally important HOW you say them.

Remember the discovery of Dr. Albert Mehrabian. The power of a message is primarily carried by the tone of voice, posture, and facial expressions.

When you declare your future don't just say words. Declare your goals with strength, volume and intense positive emotion. Stand tall with your shoulders straight and your face full of confidence and certainty.

Feelings are followers. Regardless of how you feel when you begin declaring them, your feelings will follow the confidence and authority of your tone and posture. When you communicate from a strong emotional state, your Internal Success System becomes more convinced and determined to reach the target you are aiming for.

Outside World

The outside world is the environment, structure and systems you put in place to push you towards freedom.

Please don't underestimate the importance of this aspect. The inside world is very important but without the right outside world reinforcements, you will delay or shortchange your movement towards more freedom to release your unique greatness.

Let's start with things that you directly do.

1. Be deliberate in how you use your time.

Remember, don't prioritize your schedule; rather, SCHEDULE your priorities. This means your FIRST focus is on accomplishing the "big rock" items that you have identified.

Remember that wealth, leadership and progress flow primarily from connection. Don't confuse projects with people. Manage projects, lead people. By respecting the dignity and uniqueness of each member of the team, cooperation and productivity will soar to new heights.

2. Interactions with others.

This is where this unique planning process becomes an exciting adventure. Here's a dramatic statement to consider:

Align others to serve your freedom.

Who are we talking about? This includes your employees, hired resources, your mentors and those you mentor, even your friends and relatives. Align and organize them to serve your freedom.

This may sound like an arrogant statement but really it is not. When you align other people in your life to serve your freedom, you give THEM freedom to do what they love to do and are great at doing.

You release them in their greatness to help you do those things that you hate to do, helping you to accomplish those things that drain your energy and produce little results in your life.

It is key to note the importance of rewarding their efforts, whether it is verbal praise, payment for their services, or help freeing them to do the things they love to do.

3. Make a "love and hate" list and build your team around it.

The way to build a great team in your company is first giving your employees the list of things you love to do and those things you hate to do.

Give them a copy of this list and review it with them. Make sure they understand your list and allow them to "own" that list. Have them take responsibility to help you in your freedom.

Make the list part of their new job descriptions. Their job is now primarily to serve your freedom, helping you do those things that you hate to do or are not good at doing.

As this happens, profitability will increase, productivity will improve, loyalty, happiness, strength and unity in the team will emerge.

I have suggested this process to many company presidents, pastors and other leaders and they have implemented this into their organizations. They gave employees their "Freedom Plan" as I call it.

Don't take this task on by yourself. Invite them to help you create your lists. Then allow them to invade your life and help hold you accountable to make progress on your road to freedom. Have weekly meetings to review the list and evaluate performance in helping you by taking off your plate those items on the "Things I hate" or "Stop Doing" lists.

I talked to a man recently who owned his own company. I asked him, "how is your business coming along?"

"Not too well," he said. "Our profits this year won't be near what they were last year." "What's wrong, why are the profits down this year?" I asked.

He said, "Sales are down and I am very frustrated at my job. I can't seem to get to the things that I really need to do."

I asked him if he was interested in learning how to double his profits in one year.

"Yes, I am interested, how do I do that?!!"

I briefly explained to him the Power Planning process discussed in this book. I then asked him what he really loved to do in his business. What was the one activity that gave him the most results?

He immediately knew. He said, "If I can get a client into my office to talk to them face to face, I will close 90% of them."

Then I asked him what in his job he hated to do and thought was a waste of his time. Again, he immediately knew what that was. "I hate to have to fill out all the forms and cover all the regulations. I also don't like prospecting for clients. If I could just spend all of my time closing sales in my office, I would be very happy!"

"That's exactly what this planning process can do for you. Why not design your whole office around what you are great at doing?" I asked him.

Then I explained to him the two columns – the "What I love to do" and the "What I hate to do" activities. I told him to answer the questions presented in this book and explain that list to his employees.

People are more productive and we are already seeing improvements in our sales and profits!

From that list, give them new job descriptions that would serve his freedom. I even told him to call me if he wanted me to help coach and mentor him through the process. I love to help people with this.

I saw him again awhile later and asked him, "so what did you think of what we talked about the other day?"

"I loved it!" he said. "As a matter of fact, I did what you told me to do. I made the list the same night we talked and presented it to my staff the next morning. I then allowed them to take ownership of those things I hate to do and changed their job descriptions to serve my freedom by allowing me to focus on the things I love to do.

"It's amazing! Already, there's a new level of energy and excitement in my office. People are more productive and we are already seeing improvements in our sales and profits! Tim, your planning process really produces results!! Thank you for explaining it to me!"

I applied this process to myself. I am a Certified Public Accountant. Having worked for one of the largest and most prestigious accounting firms in the world, I know how to do accounting.

Years ago, I started the Redmond Leadership Institute. This non-profit NGO has a focus on reaching out to leaders all over the world to help restore, develop and release them in their greatness to more effectively run their organizations and better serve others.

However, I found that I was bogged down doing all the accounting and clerical work. I realized that in order for this organization to make the impact that I knew it could make, I needed to move these tasks from my "to do" list to my "stop doing" list.

I had such a debate within myself about this issue because I was so good at doing this kind of work. Then I realized something.

My freedom had to come at a price.

The most important thing for me to focus on was NOT the accounting issues and the cash challenges at that time.

Instead, I had to focus on my freedom. I had to be willing to sacrifice in one area to enable me to focus on doing what I was best at doing; those activities that produced the most results.

So that's exactly what I did. We hired an accountant. At that time, it appeared that we couldn't afford to do it. But really, I couldn't afford NOT to do it. It was costing me more by not having someone on board helping to serve my freedom. Living out your freedom is always attached to the wealth creation process and the price you pay will produce bigger rewards.

As a result of unloading many of the "stop doing" items to another person, I immediately had more freedom and became much more productive in the areas that gave the Leadership Institute more results. As the productivity increased, my ability to create value and wealth increased.

Know that freedom will come with a price – but in most instances, that price is worth paying.

4. **Set up an Accountability System that you will respect even when it begins to hold you accountable.**

Without accountability, nothing gets done. Without accountability, nothing improves.

Accountability is something "other people" need (certainly not you and me!). It is something that many talk about but rarely get involved in unless they are in the driver's seat holding someone else accountable for the agreed upon results.

We want to protect those things that are our own. We don't want to open up our heart and life and show anyone where we have made mistakes. It seems too risky.

These are some of the thoughts that keep us from setting up an accountability system. However, the best run companies and highest performance people overcome their fears and subject themselves to this powerful process.

Why is it so powerful? Accountability is the key to creating your plan and it is also essential to make sure you work the plan. It will help you reach your desired destination.

Risk clarifies priorities and keeps positive pressure on the right movement and results.

Not having a system like this set up is one of the primary reasons for planning failures. Few goals and plans of significance get done unless the person creating and implementing the plan puts himself at risk. Risk clarifies priorities and keeps positive pressure on the right movement and results.

How do you put yourself at risk? How do you make sure you stay motivated when you feel like giving up? Accountability is at the heart of motivation and putting yourself at risk.

There are 3 levels of accountability.

1. **You**. The first level of accountability is with you. It is keeping promises and commitments you make to yourself. Being a person of integrity and action is necessary for sustaining long term growth. Be a person who does what you say and finishes what you start. As Stephen Covey urges, consistently win these private victories. Keeping promises you make to yourself is the key to increase the strength of your character.

2. **God**. The second level is with God. Accountability to God is determining to keep your commitments as if you made them to Him. It is also having the motivation to honor Him in WHAT you do and HOW you do it.

Every step of obedience is a step towards wealth creation. To obey is better than any sacrifice. When you submit your plan with its corresponding action items to Him, He will guide you in the implementation of your plan. Predetermine to instantly obey His leading. Obedience is key to this second level of accountability.

As a student at ORU, I listened to Oral Roberts address a leadership group I was part of. At the end of the session, he allowed us to approach him with questions.

I asked him, "what advice would you give to a young person like me aspiring to leadership?"

His eyes looked up to the ceiling in thought. Then he looked right through me as he responded. I'll never forget his words. "The key to the supernatural and setting the captives free is instant obedience."

Although he didn't use the word "leadership" in his response, he gave me his definition of leadership. Setting the captive free. Your plan and destiny is tied directly or indirectly with this as well. Instant obedience is the key to fulfilling your God-given, God-directed plan.

3. Others. The third level is with others – your mentors, managers, employees, friends, and relatives – those people who are in your inner circle.

Some ways of putting yourself at risk is by letting others know of your plan. Get them involved in helping you.

When you involve others, it puts a positive pressure on you to stay the course and never give up.

Reward. Another way of keeping yourself motivated is to give yourself a significant reward for reaching your milestones. Celebrate every time you complete an action item or reach one of the goals in the plan. Know that every successful plan is filled with numerous small steps. Keep motivation high by rewarding yourself and the team for taking each step, **Ouch!** Also exact a big enough price to pay – something that will motivate you to get back on track if you don't take constant action with your plan.

One example is to make a commitment to one of your accountability partners to give a large, agreed upon amount of money to a given charity if you slack off on keeping your commitments to accomplish your plan. Perhaps you may agree to take a cold shower for at least 45 seconds. Choose and commit to something that will motivate you to keep pursuing your plan.

The bottom line is to provide some point of pain and pleasure to stay motivated.

Give yourself some benefit to move towards and some pain or loss to want to avoid and tie that directly to staying focused on accomplishing your goals.

It is so important to set up an accountability partner or team. As John Elderideg alluded in so many words, set up an intimate ally working with God to bring out your greatness. This is someone who not only helps you in your weakness but primarily encourages you to live from your strengths.

Remember, action is what separates the good from the great – from those who wish – from those who accomplish.

The Next Step

As you come to the end of this book, you may be asking yourself, "What do I do now? What is the next step?"

You may be in a stage of your life that you are to stop immediately and make changes in how you are spending your time.

Or, you may be like most people. It is time to take inventory of your life. Perhaps you don't change what you are doing but you are to change your approach in HOW you are doing it.

Using the concept of "transference," begin to apply what you love to do in what you are currently doing. It is the way to work with your heart fully alive. By going through this planning process, you can change your approach in what you are currently doing to give you freedom to consciously and deliberately live from your heart.

But the most important point of all, as I have said before, is to take action! Use this process of planning from your heart. Answer the questions proposed throughout this book (most of which are included in the downloadable Power Planning Tools) and then begin to implement your glorious and powerful "freedom" plan that will set your heart free to enter into the abundant life that you are destined to live.

Questions to Consider, Actions to Take

Great questions precede significant progress . . . especially when you take time to think them through and write down your responses. To help you tie all the key concepts in this book, please take time to answer the following questions.

1. Are you living from your heart?

2. How would your responses be to the people you interact with most if you lived from your heart, regardless of what they said or did?

3. Are you listening to your heart? Shut down your mind for a moment and all that it is saying and even desiring. Your heart is powerful. Please take time to listen to your heart! What is your heart saying?

    Your heart is crying out to help the people closest to you. There has been a lot of pain between you and others and you are called to help bring healing and restoration to those relationships. There are dozens, hundreds, even thousands of people attached to what goes on in your heart. Please don't underestimate the power of your God-given greatness!

4. What plans or goals are you aiming at?

5. Have you written them down?

6. Have you begun to take little steps towards making them happen?

7. Are your plans so big that it would require God to intervene in order for them to come to pass? That is what He is leading you into. That is, to come into His presence and begin thinking boldly and confidently about your life and the plans for you to live out.

8. Here is the action I want you to consider taking today: Set a date with your destiny and take a moment – TODAY – to write down what is it that you want. What is your heart crying out for? What is your desire that you can unleash this powerful greatness inside of you?

9. Become a person of action. Action is what separates the successful from the mediocre. In other words, action is what separates those who have truly awakened to their greatness from those who are still asleep. Action is what is separating you from taking the next step your heart is yearning for. Take time now to write down and make visible your desires and watch your heart come alive!

10. Here's the most important question now: Are you going to apply what you have just learned? Are you going to write down answers to the questions that you have been asked?

    Become a person of action and watch your heart and life come alive as you live out your plans, goals and dreams.

    Be courageous to diligently guard, nurture and release your heart to freely and powerfully express itself.

    One of my favorite quotes is from a saint who lived in the second century. He said "The glory of God is man fully alive." Following this simple planning format can be your ticket to releasing God's glory through your life.

    Leadership is giving permission to another to become great. These are my closing words to you.

    Become uniquely great and release your greatness with all of your heart during your short time on this planet!

Planning Scriptures

These are scriptures, starting with Psalms and Proverbs from the New Living Translation of the Bible (unless otherwise noted) that speak to the subject of planning in some way.

May He grant your heart's desires and make all your plans succeed. Psa 20:4

But the LORD's plans stand firm forever; His intentions can never be shaken. Psa 33:11

O LORD my God, You have performed many wonders for us. Your plans for us are too numerous to list. You have no equal. If I tried to recite all Your wonderful deeds, I would never come to the end of them. Psa 40:5

Praise the LORD, you angels, you mighty ones who carry out His plans, listening for each of His commands. Psa 103:20

The LORD will work out His plans for my life—for Your faithful love, O LORD, endures forever. Don't abandon me, for You made me. Psa 138:8

The LORD approves of those who are good, but He condemns those who plan wickedness. Pro 12:2

The plans of the godly are just; the advice of the wicked is treacherous. Pro 12:5

Deceit fills hearts that are plotting evil; joy fills hearts that are planning peace! Pro 12:20

If you plan to do evil, you will be lost; if you plan to do good, you will receive unfailing love and faithfulness. Pro 14:22

Plans go wrong for lack of advice; many advisers bring success. (KJV . . . in the multitude of counselors, there is safety.) Pro 15:22

The LORD detests evil plans, but He delights in pure words. Pro 15:26

We can make our own plans, but the LORD gives the right answer. Pro 16:1

Commit your actions to the LORD, and your plans will succeed. Pro 16:3

We can make our plans, but the LORD determines our steps. Pro 16:9

You can make many plans, but the LORD's purpose will prevail. Pro 19:21

Plans succeed through good counsel; don't go to war without wise advice. Pro 20:18

Good planning and hard work lead to prosperity, but hasty shortcuts lead to poverty. Pro 21:5

A person who plans evil will get a reputation as a troublemaker. Pro 24:8

Do your planning and prepare your fields before building your house. Pro 24:27

Be diligent to know the state of your flocks, and attend to your herds; Pro 27:23 NKJV

She gets up before dawn to prepare breakfast for her household and plan the day's work for her servant girls. Pro 31:15

Is anything too hard for the Lord? Gen 18:14a

And Solomon, my son, learn to know the God of your ancestors intimately. Worship and serve Him with your whole heart and a willing mind. For the LORD sees every heart and knows every plan and thought. If you seek Him, you will find Him. But if you forsake Him, He will reject you forever. 1 Ch 28:9

"Every part of this plan," David told Solomon, "was given to me in writing from the hand of the LORD." 1 Ch 28:19

I slipped out during the night, taking only a few others with me. I had not told anyone about the plans God had put in my heart for Jerusalem. Neh 2:12a

The Spirit of the LORD shall rest upon Him, The Spirit of wisdom and understanding, The Spirit of counsel and might, The Spirit of knowledge and of the fear of the LORD. His delight is in the fear of the LORD, And He shall not judge by the sight of His eyes, Nor decide by the hearing of His ears; Isa 11:2-3 NKJV

I have a plan for the whole earth, a hand of judgment upon all the nations. Isa 14:26

Between the city walls, you build a reservoir for water from the old pool. But you never ask for help from the One who did all this. You never considered the One who planned this long ago. Isa 22:11

O LORD, I will honor and praise Your name, for You are my God. You do such wonderful things! You planned them long ago, and now You have accomplished them. Isa 25:1

For fools speak foolishness and make evil plans. They practice ungodliness and spread false teachings about the LORD. They deprive the hungry of food and give no water to the thirsty. Isa 32:6

But generous people plan to do what is generous, and they stand firm in their generosity. Isa 32:8

Only I can tell you the future before it even happens. Everything I plan will come to pass, for I do whatever I wish. Isa 46:10

And the LORD said, "That's right, and it means that I am watching, and I will certainly carry out all My plans." Jer 1:12

For I know the plans I have for you," says the LORD. "They are plans for good and not for disaster, to give you a future and a hope. Jer 29:11

'Call to Me, and I will answer you, and show you great and mighty things, which you do not know.' Jer 33:3

Daniel soon proved himself more capable than all the other administrators and high officers. Because of Daniel's great ability, the king made plans to place him over the entire empire. Dan 6:3

Indeed, the Sovereign LORD never does anything until He reveals His plans to His servants the prophets. Amo 3:7

The Lord now chose seventy-two other disciples and sent them ahead in pairs to all the towns and places He planned to visit. Luk 10:1

When the Spirit of truth comes, He will guide you into all truth. He will not speak on His own but will tell you what He has heard. He will tell you about the future. Joh 16:13

"So my advice is, leave these men alone. Let them go. If they are planning and doing these things merely on their own, it will soon be overthrown. Act 5:38

. . . God, who gives life to the dead and calls those things which do not exist as though they did. Rom 4:17b NKJV

For as many as are led by the Spirit of God, these are sons of God. Rom 8:14

This foolish plan of God is wiser than the wisest of human plans, and God's weakness is stronger than the greatest of human strength. 1 Co 1:25

You may be asking why I changed my plan. Do you think I make my plans carelessly? 2 Co 1:17a

For we are God's masterpiece. He has created us anew in Christ Jesus, so we can do the good things He planned for us long ago. Eph 2:10

And this is God's plan: Both Gentiles and Jews who believe the Good News share equally in the riches inherited by God's children. Both are part of the same body, and both enjoy the promise of blessings because they belong to Christ Jesus. Eph 3:6

Now all glory to God, who is able, through His mighty power at work within us, to accomplish infinitely more than we might ask or think. Eph 3:20

No, dear brothers and sisters, I have not achieved it, but I focus on this one thing: Forgetting the past and looking forward to what lies ahead, I press on to reach the end of the race and receive the heavenly prize for which God, through Christ Jesus, is calling us. Phi 3:13-14

Planning and Goal-Achieving Quotes

Proper preparation and planning produces powerful performance. Tim Redmond

Write it down. Written goals have a way of transforming wishes into wants; can'ts into cans; dreams into plans; and plans into reality. Don't just think it - ink it! Anonymous

If you don't design your own life plan, chances are you'll fall into someone else's plan. And guess what they have planned for you? Not much. Jim Rohn

A good plan violently executed now is better than a perfect plan next week. General George S. Patton

A clearly defined plan frequently reviewed empowers you to say "no!" to distractions. Tim Redmond

The best ammunition to fight poverty is a load of ambition fired with effort toward a definite goal. Anonymous

For him who has no concentration, there is no peace. Anonymous

Lack-luster, meaningless goals will remain on the shelf like a bad book. Anonymous

Blessed is he who expects nothing, for he shall never be disappointed. Alexander Pope

When planning for a year, plant corn. When planning for a decade, plant trees. When planning for life, train and educate people. Chinese Proverb

Planning is bringing the future into the present so that you can do something about it now. Alan Lakein

Goals bring focus. Tim Redmond

Circumstances may cause interruptions and delays, but never lose sight of your goal. Prepare yourself in every way you can by increasing your knowledge and adding to your experience, so that you can make the most of opportunity when it occurs. Mario Andretti

Always plan ahead. It wasn't raining when Noah built the ark. Richard C. Cushing

Bad planning on your part does not constitute an emergency on my part. Anonymous

Unless commitment is made, there are only promises and hopes; but no plans. Peter Drucker

Plans focused on just serving self breed corruption. Plans focused on serving others breed long term prosperity and stability. Tim Redmond

Good fortune is what happens when opportunity meets with planning. Thomas Edison

Make no little plans; they have no magic to stir men's blood and probably will not be realized. Make big plans; aim high in hope and work, remembering that a noble, logical diagram once recorded will not die. Daniel H. Burnham (built America's first skyscraper)

No matter how carefully you plan your goals, they will never be more than pipe dreams unless you pursue them with gusto. W. Clement Stone

Good plans shape good decisions. That's why good planning helps to make elusive dreams come true. Anonymous

It is better to take many small steps in the right direction than to make a great leap forward only to stumble backward. Anonymous

If you don't have a plan for yourself, you'll be part of someone else's. American Proverb

You can never plan the future by the past. Edmund Burke

Whatever you vividly imagine, ardently desire, sincerely believe and enthusiastically act upon must inevitably come to pass. Paul J. Meyer

If you go to work on your goals, your goals will go to work on you. If you go to work on your plan, your plan will go to work on you. Whatever good things we build end up building us. Jim Rohn

The more reasons you have for achieving your goal, the more determined you will become. Brian Tracy

The purpose of a goal is not necessarily achieving the goal itself – it is in the pursuit of the goal, we unleash the greatness within us. Tim Redmond

Walt Disney planning technique: He refused to entertain questions about whether his organizations would succeed or not. What he did do was put idea on a board outside of his office with one question on top: How can we improve this? People from all over the organization wrote suggestions down. He unlocked the creative power of his organization with this simple question.

When you pursue your goals, you will set in motion far-reaching consequences. Anonymous

What will you be doing 10 years from now? Also, what will you wish 10 years from now that you had done today? Anonymous

Having goals always causes you to act from your vision, not from your circumstances. Anonymous

You become successful the moment you start moving towards a worthwhile goal. Anonymous

You must have long range goals to keep you from being frustrated by short range failures. Charles Noble

Choosing a goal and sticking to it changes everything. Scott Reed

The tragedy of life doesn't lie in not reaching your goal. The tragedy lies in having no goal to reach. It isn't a calamity to die with dreams unfulfilled, but it is a calamity not to dream. It is not a disgrace to reach the stars, but it is a disgrace to have no stars to reach for. Not failure, but low aim, is a sin. Benjamin Mays

Don't be afraid to take a big step if one is indicated. You can't cross a chasm in two small jumps. Anonymous

You will never possess what you are unwilling to pursue. Mike Murdock

When we aren't pursuing goals or making progress in the direction of a specific desire, we begin to stagnate. Tim Redmond

The word for this hour is intensity! Pastor Billy Joe Daugherty

Life is either a daring adventure or nothing at all. Helen Keller

I am appalled at the aimlessness of most people's lives. Fifty percent don't pay any attention to where they're going. Forty percent are undecided and will go in any direction. Only ten percent know what they want and even all of them don't go towards it. Katherine A. Porter

In order to do an urgent and important work, two things are necessary: a definite plan and not quite enough time. Anonymous

Set aside a little time at least once a year, to decide, at least where you are going, what your priorities, ambitions and aspirations are. Anonymous

Nothing is as necessary for success as a single-minded pursuit of an objective. Fred Smith, Founder of Federal Express

Focus requires one to be selective. Tim Redmond

If your desires be endless, your cares and fears will be so, too. Thomas Fuller

Give a man health and a course to steer, and he'll never stop to trouble about whether he's happy or not. George Bernard Shaw

There are too many people in too many cars in too much of a hurry going too many directions to get nowhere for nothing. John Mason

Four steps to achievement: Plan purposefully. Prepare prayerfully. Proceed positively. Pursue persistently. William A. Ward

In the long run, men hit only what they aim at. Therefore, though they should fail immediately, they had better aim at something high. Henry David Thoreau

By failing to prepare, you are preparing to fail. Benjamin Franklin

Focus comes when you have clearly answered the why of your goal. Tim Redmond

Thoroughness characterizes all successful men. Genius is the art of taking infinite pains. All great achievement has been characterized by extreme care, infinite, painstaking, even to the minutest detail. Elbert Hubbard

Reduce your plan to writing. The moment you complete this, you will have definitely given concrete form to the intangible desire. Napoleon Hill

It's not the plan that is important, it's the planning. Graeme Edwards

See the things you want as already yours. Think of them as yours, as belonging to you, as already in your possession. Robert Collier

I am looking for a lot of men who have an infinite capacity to not know what can't be done. Henry Ford

Many people fail in life, not for lack of ability or brains or even courage but simply because they have never organized their energies around a goal. Elbert Hubbard

Emptiness is a symptom that you are not living creatively. You either have no goal that is important enough to you, or you are not using your talents and efforts in a striving toward an important goal. Maxwell Maltz

Act like you expect to get into the end zone. Joe Paterno, Penn State coach

Goals give you more than a reason to get up in the morning; they are an incentive to keep you going all day. Goals tend to tap the deeper resources and draw the best out of life. Harvey Mackay

All successful people have a goal. No one can get anywhere unless he knows where he wants to go and what he wants to be or do. Norman Vincent Peale

You are never too old to set another goal or to dream a new dream. Les Brown

Man is a goal seeking animal. His life only has meaning if he is reaching out and striving for his goals. Aristotle

Give me a stock clerk with a goal and I'll give you a man who will make history. Give me a man with no goals and I'll give you a stock clerk. J.C. Penney

A goal is a dream with a deadline. Napoleon Hill

Goals that are not written down are just wishes. Anonymous

Goals are dreams we convert to plans and take action to fulfill. Zig Ziglar

An average person with average talents and ambition and average education, can outstrip the most brilliant genius in our society, if that person has clear, focused goals. Mary Kay Ash

Endnotes

1. *Chicken Soup for the Soul*

2. Ibid

3. Matthew 6:33

4. Luke 17:21

5. Romans 14:17

6. Isaiah 55:8-9

7. Colossians 3:15

8. Nehemiah 8:10

9. II Peter 1:4

10. Mark 11:24

11. *The One Minute Millionaire: The Enlightened Way to Wealth*

12. *7 Habits of Highly Effective People*

13. Quoted by Gil Bailey in John Elderidge's book, *Wild at Heart*

Business and Leadership Mastermind Club

We specialize in helping leaders like you focus and take action to increase your wealth-creation/business and leadership capacities.

By combining spiritual insights with practical "real life" application on a consistent basis, this unique coaching program brings transformation to your organization and life.

Expect results BIG results! Increased income. Greater peace, joy and freedom.

Be part of a powerful and creative group of leaders who want to expand the Kingdom of God in practical and powerful ways as they . . . Prosper on Purpose for a Purpose

Four Benefits of This Growth Acceleration Program:

1. **Monthly LIVE MEETINGS** via phone with Tim and selected experts covering strategies, mindsets and world-class practices to help you grow your business and develop your leadership effectiveness. Includes Q/A, live interaction, and specific application exercises. The Learning Process Tim incorporates is VERY effective!

2. **Recording of the LIVE Event** to listen to as often as you wish - download it to your MP3 player!

3. **Downloadable Tool** to immediately apply the concepts in each of the LIVE Events. This is key to maximizing your results for each of these powerful training sessions.

4. **Downloadable Training Manual** of the entire session to review and study, including clarifying "life application" worksheets to fill in. Each Training Manual is chocked full of application exercises, motivating quotes and key scriptures relating to the topic.

Here's what some of Mastermind Club Members are saying about this program:

Very powerful! Tim covers pertinent subjects that I need to grow my business now.

—Harold Friesen, Business Owner

How is Tim different? He generates great horsepower from his unique background – accounting/business, psychology, spiritual . . . plus building and selling a successful high-growth company. His vast experience and wisdom translates to deep psychological and spiritual understanding of me and my staff and growth for my company!

—Betsi Bixby, President – Meridian

The first session was worth the entire year's investment!

—Ron Vaughn, GC and Developer

To find out how you can enroll in this personal and professional growth acceleration program, please email us at

connect@redmondleadership.org

or call us directly at 918.298.7766 (US) or go to the website (www.redmondleadership.org) and click the Mastermind Club under Learning Products.

4 Free Downloadable Power Planning Tools

To help you immediately apply the powerful principles contained in this book, we are providing you with 4 interactive tools formatted in the Adobe Acrobat PDF format.

To get access to these valuable tools, please follow these instructions:

1. Go to the website page:

http://redmondleadership.org/site/view/73155_OrderFreeTools.pml

2. From this webpage, click to our store and process the request. You will note that the amount is set to zero. After completing this short process, you will be provided the download link to have access to the 4 Power Planning Tools. Download the 4 files.

3. Begin using these tools for your planning process!

About the Author

Tim Redmond is an expert in bringing transformation to individuals and organizations through his innovative, prophetic and often humorous training approach on wealth creation, rapid-growth mindsets and strategies, high impact leadership, and building top performance teams.

Tim grew a leading high tech company from two employees to over 450 employees, generating millions in sales and profits.

After selling the business to a Fortune 500 company, Tim created the Redmond Leadership Institute to train leaders in business, church, education and government to impart his productive insights he has gained from successfully running and consulting a number of businesses and ministries. Individuals have paid up to $50,000 for a 5-day business growth intensive that Tim conducted.

Based on the powerful results he achieves, Tim has become a popular business, church and conference speaker internationally. Tim and the Leadership Institute frequently work in developing countries to reach, restore and release leaders to tap the unlimited potential in their organizations, communities and countries.

He has also worked with Dr. John Maxwell and the Equip team to train hundreds of leaders in Bogota, Colombia.

Tim graduated with a Bachelor of Science degree (with Honors) in Accounting and earned his Certified Public Accounting (CPA) status. He worked at PriceWaterhouseCoopers for a number of years before joining Tax and Accounting Software Corporation (TAASC) and Intuit, where he has served for over 15 years.

He is happily married to Sandra and has 4 "leaders in training" (Matthew, Robert, Joshua, and Andrea).

Tim has published books and numerous training CD seminars designed to strength and expand the leadership and wealth creation capacities of those he addresses.

Some of the Business and Leadership Training Materials Tim offers include:

- Wealth Manifesto – Releasing Your Unique Power to Create Wealth
- Emotions of Money
- Discovering Your Greatness (companion audio to this book)
- Leadership's Biggest Battle
- Leadership from the Heart
- PeaceMaker – Strategies for Resolving Conflicts and Building Powerful Relationships
- Money and Marriage
- Real Life Marriage – An Honest Conversation Between A Husband and Wife
- Personal and Professional Accelerated Growth Packages –
  - Power of Focus – The Fuel that Drives Progress
  - Building Unshakeable Confidence
  - Make Better Decisions
  - Profitably Managing Your Emotional State
  - Key Strategies for Growing Your Business Now
  - Tapping the FLOW of Peak Productivity

We at Redmond Leadership Institute (RLI) trust you enjoyed this book and found practical applications to your life. Please call, write, or email us to let us know how this book has helped you.

To order multiple copies of this book, please contact RLI directly.

Also, please contact us to have Tim and/or Sandy Redmond address your company, church or conference and work directly with you and your leadership team.

For power-packed, motivating and clarifying "thought bursts" (and to stay in touch with me!) follow me on Twitter.

www.twitter.com/timredmond

Redmond Leadership Institute
PO Box 703052
Tulsa, OK 74170, USA.
918.298.7766

Email: connect@redmondleadership.org

Visit our website at www.RedmondLeadership.org to receive free monthly Leadership Lessons and practical wealth creation ideas. Please know that your email address will be kept in the strictest confidence.